The Book of
SWANAGE

Portrait of a Dorset Seaside Town

RODNEY LEGG

HALSGROVE

First published in Great Britain in 2001

This book is dedicated to the memory of
J. BERNARD CALKIN

Frontispiece photograph: *The postman brings 'Good*
tidings from Swanage' (with a miniature set of photographs
opening from the white flap on his back).

British Library Cataloguing-in-Publication Data
A CIP record for this title is available from the British Library

ISBN 1 84114 111 9

HALSGROVE
PUBLISHING, MEDIA AND DISTRIBUTION

Halsgrove House
Lower Moor Way
Tiverton, Devon EX16 6SS
Tel: 01884 243242
Fax: 01884 243325
email: sales@halsgrove.com
website: www.halsgrove.com

Printed and bound in Great Britain by Bookcraft Ltd., Midsomer Norton

PROLOGUE

As Enid Blyton used to say, 'I always spend my holidays in Swanage'. I quote the line when cold-callers offer their latest 'free holiday' scam to some ghastly resort of the English abroad. My alternative has always been to look west, though not too far, and Swanage has been my special place on our own holiday coast for as long as I can remember. That was when I was still reading Noddy and we crossed green waters by paddle-steamer from Bournemouth with porpoises playing alongside. Then it became an objective by land and alone, by cycle from age 11 onwards, then steam train, and eventually on foot. That could be made more challenging by following flashing navigation lights through the night.

Swanage and Purbeck offered rugged scenery that was the front-line to the sea, with fast-moving weather, and colours far stronger than the drab greys further west. Some people still had real jobs and did things with pieces of the planet in ways that were positively primeval. Exuberant architecture from higher up that craft included the best of London's cast-offs. I collected the wording of the stone inscriptions around George Burt's Durlston Park Estate as time and weather took their toll.

Ancient history embraced a kindly retired headmaster and archaeologist. As a 13-year-old this author was slipped surplus antiquities by J. Bernard Calkin from museum cupboards and stimulated an interest that now almost earns a living. I wish I could show him my Roman altar, in Purbeck marble, and discuss the find spot. On the cliffs I was a natural free-climber, ambushing surprised real climbers with a camera lens, and having a Wessex rescue helicopter almost clipping the rocks above my head as a winchman dangled down to a completely safe me, who provided the perfect idiot for a training exercise. This was my adventure playground.

I even explored its underground recesses, crawling down holes in the quarrylands. It was a landscape being lost. Railing against philistine destruction, and finding no one to listen, I founded *Dorset: The County Magazine* to fight for Purbeck in 1968, campaigning to protect endangered archaeology and unappreciated industrial relics, and protest the ploughing of a profusion of orchids on Ballard Down. 'I do not think any place in the world ever grew such wild flowers,' Victorian author Mrs J.E. Panton wrote of Swanage.

Things started to change for the better when Dorset County Council created Durlston County Park in 1974, and Ralph Bankes bequeathed all his lands to the National Trust on his death in 1981. Mrs Panton would have been delighted that English Nature has declared recreated wild-flower meadows to be 'the best in Britain'. Subsequent consolidation by conservation owners has given us a Jurassic coast that is now set to win the kudos of World Heritage Site status.

'Sunny Swanage', I always call it, because my exertions with a camera require blue-sky days, and if I decide it is too dull and dismal to leave home and travel south then I am bound to hear on the midnight news that 'the sunniest place in Britain was Swanage in Dorset, with 13 hours of unbroken sunshine'. Even Swanage suburbia is under some sort of self-control and for the most part stays out of sight, seldom striking one as a town of 9000 inhabitants, rising to 25 000 in high summer.

'Welcome to Swanage' beside the Ulwell Gap through the Purbeck Hills.

My past words started with *Purbeck Island* in 1972 and were given new impetus in 1999 with the position of founding editor of *Purbeck: The Country Magazine*. In between I have researched much else, some of which has been expanded here, and friends in Swanage have contributed other nuggets. I am particularly grateful for encouragement from author Merle Chacksfield, architect David Lewer, and veteran reporter and Swanage sage George Willey of Cluny Crescent, and father of Wolf of the Red Lion, who has supplied sparkling anecdotes. The initial idea for the book, and then the necessary doses of deadline discipline, came from the publishers at Halsgrove House where Naomi Cudmore and Sharon O'Inn have assembled a library of such studies with loving care.

Here the design and layout has been by Sharon while Naomi applied the editorial skills.

As for the photographs, in 1983 Norah Kaye gave me free access to the archives of Thomas Powell, who was Walter Pouncy's employee in Swanage in late Victorian times, and those of his son, William Powell (1882–1973), who was Mrs Kaye's father. Others have since selected me as a virtual museum for their treasures. Their generosity has resulted in a personal collection that now comprises 320 Swanage postcards mainly from the Edwardian period. These days the only problem – with words as well as images – is what to leave out. My hope is that you, in sunny Swanage, will enjoy the surviving selection.

Right: 'A Greeting from Swanage' from the days before Hitler when the Swastika was 'A mascot to bring you luck'.

Below: 'A Gallant Rescue' in a classic Raphael Tuck 'Oilette' posted to Miss Rosemary Neil Smith in Hoddesdon in 1916 with the message 'Puzzle III, find Mummy. Love and kisses from Daddy'.

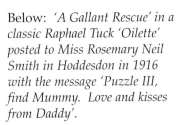

Edwardian watercolour of St Mary's Church from the former
Mill Pond Farm, painted by Ernest Haslehust.

Above: *Looking north-east from the High Road at Court Hill in 1850 to Carrant's Court Farm (left),
Northbrook Farm (centre), and the cluster of buildings around St Mary's Church, painted by C.M. Colvile.*

Below: *Northwards along the beach to Cliff Cottage and Shore Villa
in an otherwise empty north Swanage in 1850, painted by 'A.T.'.*

CONTENTS

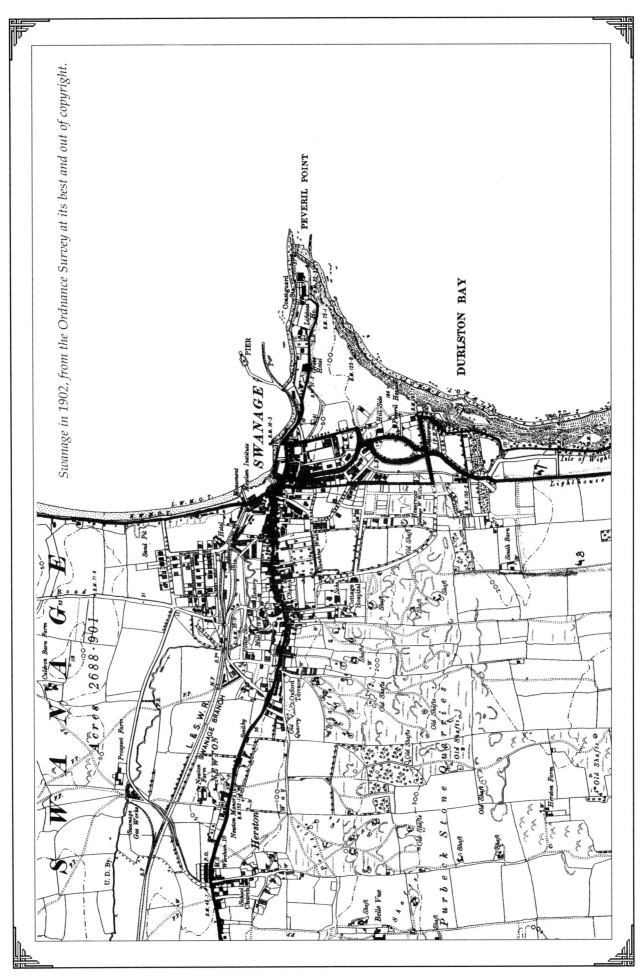

Swanage in 1902, from the Ordnance Survey at its best and out of copyright.

Chapter 1

EARTH AND DINOSAURS

Purbeck continues to produce more dinosaur footprints than any other area in the British Isles and can now claim more than everywhere else added together. One of the major finds of recent times was on the edge of the 19th-century Townsend Quarries, on the southern side of Swanage, beneath a building plot that became No. 19 Townsend Road. David Selby, a builder, cracked open a stone and found a distinct three-toed dinosaur footprint. This was in the Lanning vein of the Purbeck Beds, and Paul Ensom of Dorset County Museum carried out an excavation in August 1981 which revealed large hollows, pushed into the stone, which indicated that the dinosaur had been lying down in what was then stiff mud. A total of 17 'tridactyl' prints were extracted from an area of 125 square yards.

The creature had 'walked on its hind legs, placing one foot in front of the other,' as extra-terrestrials may one day write of us.

The fossil reptile is usually identified as a Megalosaurus, though some have been from previously unknown species, and *Purbeckopus pentactyles* was named from a unique set of 6-inch prints found in a quarry to the west of the quarrying hamlet of Acton. One long set of 26 Megalosaurus prints, covering a length of more than 70 feet, was found in 1962 in E.W. Suttle's Mutton Hole Quarry at Herston, with some now being displayed in the forecourt of the British Museum of Natural History, in Kensington. J. Bernard Calkin had described 14 Iguanodon footprints from the same Herston workings in 1933.

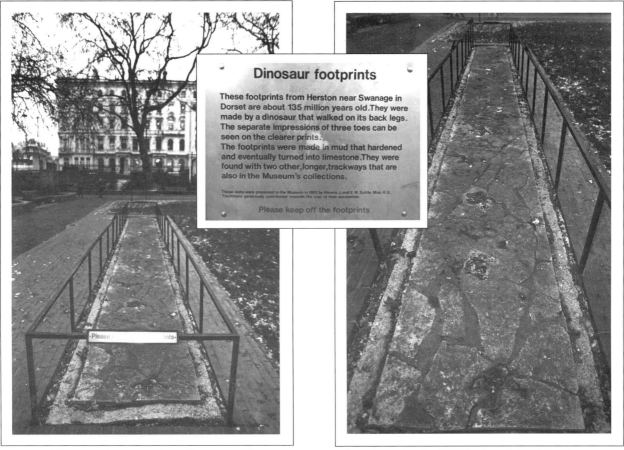

Dinosaur footprints

These footprints from Herston near Swanage in Dorset are about 135 million years old. They were made by a dinosaur that walked on its back legs. The separate impressions of three toes can be seen on the clearer prints.
The footprints were made in mud that hardened and eventually turned into limestone. They were found with two other, longer, trackways that are also in the Museum's collections.

These slabs were presented to the Museum in 1963 by Messrs J. and E.W. Suttle. Miss H.G. Trechmann generously contributed towards the cost of their excavation.

Please keep off the footprints

Dinosaur footprints from Herston at Swanage, presented to the nation in 1963 by J. and E.W. Suttle and re-laid in London, beside the entrance to the National History Museum, South Kensington.

Accessible footprints on Peveril Downs at Swanage.

The remarkable story of dinosaur *Dorsetochelyn delairi* took place in the mid 1970s when science caught up with a fossil which had been in the Dorset County Museum collection at Dorchester since 1908. It had come from the Purbeck Beds at Swanage. Only the upper part of a turtle skull was visible and the rest of the animal's head was embedded in stone. Rather than risk damaging it by removal, the skull and the remainder of the fossil were left in the lump of limestone.

Using an acetic acid solution technicians at the Zoology Museum in Cambridge dissolved away the matrix of encrustation. This released the skull and its intricate lower side could then be examined for the first time. It was only the second turtle skull known from the Isle of Purbeck and the scientists soon found they were dealing not only with a new species but a new genus as well. It shares features with two other turtle families and is thought to be an evolutionary link between them.

The animal was alive 100 million years ago when southern England was covered by tropical swampland on the edge of a warm sea. The gradual drift of tectonic plates had yet to bring this land into cooler climes. The skull has been called *Dorsetochelyn delairi*, with its specific name being a tribute to Purbeck fossil collector Justin Delair.

About 65 million years ago the first small shrew-like mammals were given an opportunity to occupy niches from which the ubiquitous dinosaurs had been removed. These prototype mammals were helped by their small size in pulling through the disaster that ended the dinosaur epoch. After the climatic catastrophe, mammals ruled the world, and no traces of dinosaurs are found in later rocks. Yet neither are there any fossils in the rocks to explain the sequence of intermediaries between the reptiles and their successors, the mammals. Clearly, the mammals did not come about through gradual evolution, but erupted suddenly as a result of some dramatic interruption to the order of the world.

That Purbeck holds the clues to the truth is apparent from the reptilian evidence in the quarrylands and also from the fact that one of the earlier mammal beds in the country is on the cliffs at Durlston Bay where scattered remains of marsupials were discovered by W.R. Brodie (1830–76) and Charles Wilcox in 1854. They show the start of the advanced stages of air-breathing mammalian development that have led to ourselves; though not what created the marsupials. Mammal bones from the basal bed above Durlston Bay were excavated by Samuel Husband Beccles (1814–90) who rented No. 4 Victoria Terrace, employed a dozen workmen, and spent most of 1856 digging a pit in the top of the cliff, a few yards north from where Durlston Castle now stands. The rent was £200 and the men's wages totalled £150. A further £40 was spent on acquiring Brodie's specimens. On being taken home they were meticulously cleaned and drawn and would be given extensive coverage in the *Illustrated London News* of Boxing Day in 1857. Beccles could claim 'no less than 27 species of marsupial animals, about 16 of which were then entirely new to science.' They were 'almost the only mammals known to have existed before the Tertiary period' and would stoke the great creation debate erupting with publication of Charles Darwin's theory of evolution.

Though the classic landform geology of Purbeck, Dorset and Southern England is to be found to the west, condensed around Lulworth Cove, Swanage Bay sections and exposes the same rocks in wider measures from north to south. The chalk ridge of the Purbeck Hills dips into the sea at Ballard Point. Next come the colourful mixture of Wealden sands and clays along the bed into which the broad valley has been cut. Shep's Hollow was its scenic gash at north Swanage.

South-eastwards are the stones for which Purbeck has been famous for two millennia, being the ledges of so-called marble and other shelly limestones which shelve into the waves from Peveril Point. Then comes the second of Swanage's two indented shorelines, forming an east-facing arc around Durlston Bay, followed by the best man-made cuts through the stone-belt at Tilly Whim Caves. Here the coast turns west, at Anvil Head, into vertical cliffs beside the stone plateau which eventually juts out into the English Channel at St Alban's Head to form the south-western view.

Durlston as a placename derives from the former feature of its landform geology. As with the Thurlstone in Devon and Durdle Door at Lulworth ('th' sounds being rendered as 'd' in the Dorset dialect) the name Durlston means 'pieced rock'. There was a blow-hole on the headland, drawn by Philip Brannon about 1860 and apparently blocked by falling debris when Durlston Castle was built. It spouted with water propelled by compressed air during regular wave action. This column was shown by Brannon as

Left: *Explosive sea, looking north-east from Anvil Point to Tilly Whim Caves (left) and Durlston Head, showing another aspect of seaside Swanage.*

Right: *Punfield Cove and the northern sweep of Swanage Bay, around to Ballard Point.*

Left and Below: *Industrial archaeology at Godlingston, with Swanage Brick and Tile Works having produced hand-made products on the same site for three centuries, its buildings being photographed by Colin Graham in 1985.*

reaching the height of about 25 feet above sea level. He also depicted the surrounding geology of 'transverse faults and contorted beds'.

Another vanished feature was at the other end of the Swanage shoreline. There used to be a large pond at the foot of Ballard Cliff, now a National Trust property, and the farmer from Whitecliff Farm kept swans on it. William Masters Hardy recounted a tradition that Punfield Pond, north-east of Shep's Hollow, had been frequently visited by King John who had a hunting lodge on Windmill Knap, above Tom Burnham's Oak. If the Swanage placename derives from a swannery then this could either have been in the creek – the former backwater of The Brook estuary – or at Punfield. Boulders that contained the pond were broken up by quarrymen, in about 1705, to make up for shortages in shipments required for repairing dikes in the Netherlands.

Punfield retains considerable interest for geologists. It is highly fossiliferous and contains the Punfield marine band which has Spanish affinities. This lies in the cretaceous layers, of the final Mesozoic period, when the lower greensand and colourful Wealden sands were accumulating in what were then tropical waters. These beds of white, blue, brown and grey sands are mixed with red, purple, brown, blue and green clays.

Windmill Knap is rising ground at the 200-feet contour just west of Burnham's Lane at Godlingston. It has two claims to distant historical features though nothing is now to be seen on the ground. The ruins of a tower windmill were visible in Victorian times and reputed to have been built with the stone from a ranger's lodge of the medieval Purbeck Forest. The walls of the latter were still standing in 1618 and, as with a similar hunting lodge on Creech Barrow Hill six miles to the west, which does still have visible foundations, it is said by local legend to have been built by King John. East of The Knap, the memory of the windmill is also perpetuated by Windmill Barn.

Since the 19th century this landscape has provided the natural ingredients for the products of Swanage Brick and Tile Works, inland between Godlingston and Ulwell, which remains one of the few brickworks still producing hand-made bricks in Britain. Before being mixed and used the chosen Wealden clays and sands are stacked in heaps in the yard to 'weather'. The resultant products are highly distinctive both in the making and appearance. Slight irregularities make for character that is absent in the standard sameness of their machine-made counterparts.

The technique of hand-moulding bricks is such that the maker leaves his signature in the form of a pattern of creases in the face of the brick. At the works they always know who made each one. They are left to dry gently in tunnels for just over a week, during which time each brick loses a pint of water by evaporation, before the setters fill their kilns. This is also done by hand.

The kilns stack 45 000 bricks and are fired for 85 hours, using 3000 gallons of oil, at a temperature approaching 1200 degrees centigrade. It then takes ten days for the kilns to cool before opening. The coloration of a brick will depend upon its position in the kiln rather than the ingredients, with the darkest brick – which the works markets as 'Dorset Blue' – coming from the hottest part of the kiln. They are exceedingly hard and dappled blue with permanent colour that does not weather out. Light reds predominate towards the bottom of the kiln. Analysis by the Building Research Station proved them to be strong and 'resistant to frost even under severe conditions', such as in parapets, and 'very low' in soluble salt content with 'negligible' leaching or efflorescence.

Godlingston Brickworks was owned by the Bankes Estate and came into National Trust ownership in 1982. It was sold in 1988 to Redland Brick Company. In 1995 the firm, which was employing 24 people, bought extraction rights on an adjoining 7-acre field.

Rainfall at Ulwell which seeps to more than 80 feet below the hamlet is lost for abstraction purposes as it runs into a fault which drains the southern side of Ballard Down in an eastward direction and issues from the sea bed between the Grand Hotel at the northern end of Swanage Beach and the white cliffs of Ballard Point. Fresh water bubbles up in quantities in a flow that remained substantial as the rest of the county became parched in the double drought years of 1975–76. A century earlier the bargemen and shippers carrying stone from Swanage Bay knew the precise spot and lowered casks into the sea to fill them with their drinking water.

Chapter 2

BARROWS AND BEGINNINGS

Ulwell Barrow, the largest surviving Bronze-Age burial mound on Ballard Down, with a gas-lamp obelisk having been set in its side in Victorian times.

As with so many Dorset towns and villages, the earliest visible history as seen from Swanage is strung along the skyline as a succession of Bronze-Age burial mounds, dating from the Wessex Culture of Stonehenge vintage, between 2100 and 1500BC. Of the eight on Ballard Down, the western one beside the obelisk is the best preserved. Known as the Ulwell Barrow, the 6-foot-high bowl barrow was dug by Victorian antiquary John Austen in 1857. It is 74 feet in diameter and surrounded with a ditch which is 12 feet wide. Austen found a trussed-up skeleton in a chalk-cut grave, with a fine red-ware cup which would have held a drink for the chieftain's journey into the after-world. An antler in the filling showed how the grave had been dug. A later skeleton, urn fragments, and a cremation had been inserted into the mound over subsequent centuries.

To the east, also on National Trust land, the barrows have fared less well. They were also excavated by John Austen and his barrow diggers between 1851 and 1857. The mounds were then quite sizeable but those in the eastern cluster were damaged during the Second World War, apparently for the construction of a coastal radar station, and all were denuded by post-war ploughing for cereals, which was stopped when Whiteway Farm was bought by the National Trust in 1976.

As with the Ulwell Barrow there was a single crouched skeleton beneath each mound and pieces of antler-pick which had been used to quarry the chalk. The mounds had then been re-used later in the Bronze Age for the insertion of cremation burials. The urns containing these had largely disintegrated. There was also the burial of a child in a pit that had been cut into the chalk.

There are also two barrow-like mounds on Godlingston Hill, known as the Giant's Grave and Giant's Trencher, which overlook the Ulwell Gap. Both were excavated by the Victorian antiquary John Austen and found to be empty. They might have been cenotaphs, as memorials to aristocrats whose bodies could not be recovered, from battle or the sea.

Roman working places are densely concentrated across the Isle of Purbeck, with workshops being part of the villa complex at Bucknowle, on the Church Knowle side of the Copper Bridge beside Corfe Common. Similar buildings have been excavated at Woodhouse, west of Studland village, and Purbeck marble from Wilkswood and beyond was worked at Norden and found its way across the province of Britannia. It would have been shipped out. Purbeck gravestones and other carvings with inscriptions are known from Dorchester and Silchester to London and Colchester. Dozens have been recorded but many more exist, such as the altar to Fortuna from an undisclosed Dorset location that is before me as I write, beside a Purbeck marble horse-and-rider carving from Bere Regis.

The sheltered waters of Poole Harbour would have been a far safer export point than the exposed shoreline of Swanage Bay. The harbour also had a string of pottery kilns producing bulk loads of wares for the legions on Hadrian's Wall. On the other hand some of Swanage and much of Durlston has since 'gone off to sea' as the old-timers used to tell me.

Nonetheless, there is talk of Roman finds in the vicinity of Whitecliff Farm and David Henstridge found a hoard of coins in cliff slippage below the Grand Hotel in 1961. They are an unusual mixture of periods and places, of the sort that a mariner might collect in the Mediterranean, and hide on coming ashore in Shep's Hollow for a return that never happened.

Romano-British graves abound, from eight skeletons beside Lighthouse Road, close to La Belle Vue Restaurant, found in June 1904, to 60 cists and other inhumations at Shepherd's Farm, discovered in 1949 and 1982. Their alignment was in the Christian east-west convention but that also applies to the Romano-Christian cemetery beside Poundbury Camp at Dorchester. Both graveyards remained in use in post-Roman times. An earlier skeleton in a wooden coffin set in a stone cist, with a brooch dated to circa AD150, was found in Atlantic Road in 1953. Numerous skeletons, including the skulls Cyril Parsons lined up along the wall of the Tithe Barn, have been found in the vicinity of St Mary's Parish Church. 'You would expect heads around a medieval graveyard,' J. Bernard Calkin told me, 'but they could well be much earlier. I excavated a Roman lady, buried with care but decapitated after death, in the foundations of Studland Church. Even Wimborne Minster, the great Saxon church, has a slab of Roman mosaic floor preserved in the nave.'

There was a seamless transition from Roman to Saxon times, along the South Coast anyway, but terror came to Dorset from the sea, in acts of piracy, and Viking longships plundered Portland in 840. Better news was reported from Purbeck but the legendary Battle of Swanage Bay probably never happened. Or, rather, it was waged and won by the elements rather than man, in a significant turning of the tide against Viking invaders in 877. Professor F.M. Stenton, in his *Anglo-Saxon England*, came to the conclusion that there was no battle at all, but that a Danish fleet – taking reinforcements to raiders laying siege to Exeter – 'was destroyed by a storm off Swanage'. The contemporary *Anglo-Saxon Chronicle* records that 120 ships were lost. A dramatic account of the loss was incorporated in *The Namesake* by C. Walter Hodges.

'Swanawic,' in the *Anglo-Saxon Chronicle*, is the first recorded form of the Swanage placename. The origin of the name has been given as 'herdsmen's dairy farm' – showing ignorance of 'wic' and salt-making – and placename historian A.D. Mills concedes that 'swan is equally possible for the first element, in which case the name might mean swannery.' The heart of what became the town, then as now, must have been around the clear springs that became the Mill Pond with the Parish Church adjacent. The mill-wheel long ago stopped turning and business ceased in 1928.

Masterful Walter Pouncy composition of about 1895, with the two girls and boy balancing his shot of the Mill Pond, looking north from Church Hill to summertime elms beyond The Brook.

Victorian Seaside

Above: *A pair of cottages at the mouth of The Brook, painted in the early-19th century, before being washed away in a gale on 29 December 1848.*

Above: *Looking north-west from Purbeck House during the 1870s, across Tilly Mead to Eastbrook Farm (left of centre) and Ballard Down, before the building of the railway and Station Road.*

Left: *View from the Royal Victoria Hotel, in one of the earliest landscape photographs taken at Swanage, looking across to Ballard Point with the 1859-built pier kiosk glimpsed in the foreground (left) and the north wall of Marine Villa (right).*

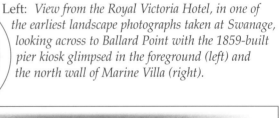

Right: *The view south-eastwards from the first pier, in 1864, across to the Coastguard Station and Lookout (left) on Peveril Point, commanded by Frederick Hildebrand Stevens RN.*

Left: The Rose *at the stone quay (right) in a Philip Brannon print of 1856, with the Royal Victoria Hotel (behind), the Rookery and Seymer Road (centre), Marine Villa (foreground) and The Grove (left).*

Victorian Seaside

*Contrasting summer and winter views southwards along the pier approach in
two Walter Pouncy studies of 1894–95, before the building of the new pier.*

Victorian Seaside

Above: *View from the church tower in the 1870s, towards Ballard Down with Northbrook Road crossing the middle distance, passing Northbrook Farm, and the 1865-built de Moulham Villas being the single modern building (right).*

Above: *New Swanage, north from the White House (left) around Swanage Bay to the 1898-built Grand Hotel (right), with bathing machines between, in a photograph of c.1900.*

Right: *Bathing machines, north of the White House, in a view looking southwards along Beech Rd in 1883, when there were still stone bankers on this side of the Mowlem Institute.*

New Swanage, from beyond the White House, to White's bathing machine (left of centre), and the fast-growing suburb beneath Ballard Down, in 1900.

Victorian Seaside

Southwards around the central section of Swanage Bay from the Mowlem Institute (middle right) to the Royal Victoria Hotel (centre) and Belvedere House (above), with Peveril Downs beyond the trees, c.1895.

Left: *The Captain Birdseye of his day, at the turn of the 20th century, was John Go-to-bed who lived with his donkey in Hop-about Lane.*

Flag-decked White House, the home of David and Thirza Hibbs, facing the sands from Beach Road, in about 1900.

A closer view from the White House (foreground, right) to the Mowlem Institute (right, centre) with Mowlem's Column standing between it and the bathing machine, in about 1895.

Victorian Seaside

Albion Place (right) and the distinctive three-storey Round House, with the shop of toy dealer James Haysom, at the junction of the High Street and Institute Road, seen in about 1890.

Thomas Stockley's coffee tavern and fruiterer's shop, opposite the Ship Inn, with the board advertising attractions on the Durlston Park Estate which opened to the public in 1887.

Channel view over roofs of the eastern High Street with John Mowlem's Observatory being the flat-topped addition to his home at No. 2 Victoria Terrace, photographed in 1885.

Old Bank House, formerly housing the branch office of the Dorsetshire Bank, was the home of James Clifton in the 1890s.

Drainage work in the 1890s between the White Swan (far right) and Albion Place, with the stone bankers visible in the background (centre).

Victorian Seaside

Above: *Wheelwright in action, at the Smithy on the north side of the High Street opposite Mount Pleasant Lane in the 1890s, the water causing the red-hot iron rim to contract around the spokes.*

Below: *Cart approaching the Mowlem Institute along Station Road, photographed from the county bridge that carried Institute Road over what was still an open brook, in about 1890.*

Swanage historians, from William Masters Hardy to David Lewer, have puzzled over the enigma of the age and sturdiness of the church tower, with walls nearly five feet thick, and as plain as they come in a land of stonemasons. 'Was it a fortified building?' Lewer asks himself, and comes up with an intriguing explanation of the nearby Paradise name, where the post-war rectory stands, that this derives from the French word 'parados' – for the defensive mound protecting a fortification from the rear. The lower three storeys of the tower, with massive corner stones laid alternately long and short, and thin strips of stone have been claimed as a late Saxon work of circa AD1000. There are also arrow-slit windows and a blocked-up door or window in the east wall of the first storey which has triangular arching that is said to show Saxon characteristics. The top storey was added in 1620 and now houses eight bells.

In this context the church's position is relevant, as it stands beside The Brook which has its only non-culverted section in the next-door grounds of Swanwic House, which was the old rectory. Until relatively recent times this was a wide, tidal backwater, and its lowest downstream crossing point, from Northbrook Road, was opposite the Parish Church. This is not proof of any strategic purpose, as it would also be logical – for attendance at services and the practicalities of bringing coffins – to locate the church in a sensible position that was also accessible from the northern half of the parish.

Church architectural historian Fred Pitfield, in *Purbeck Parish Churches*, regards this speculation over a fortified refuge as 'rather fanciful'. He proves that the original building, in line with the outer walls of the tower, extended eastwards with a long and narrow single-cell nave and chancel. That was the typical style for a chapel which he dates to the 13th century; adding the tower to the plan in the 14th. Another sceptic, Frederick Leigh Colvile in 1853, regarded the 'parochial fortress' suggestion as fanciful and pointed out that Swanage people tended to back-date their history: 'The town is said to be very ancient, and popularly reputed to be built before the time of Christ!' He thought the 'parochial fortress' suggestion was wishful thinking and that 'the date of its erection may be in the 12th century'.

Swanwich or Sandwich, its common name in the Middle Ages, became a place of national strategic importance. Placename enthusiasts have made a meal of both forms but either 'swan' or 'sand' is logical enough, and the localised 'wich' element in and around Poole Harbour is for a place involved in the making or selling of salt, which was extracted from evaporated sea water. It is the same 'wich' as Droitwich and Nantwich (rock salt) and Ipswich and Norwich (sea salt).

Swanage appears with Wareham and Poole in the trio of south-east Dorset coastal towns in a defence map from the time of Henry VIII, when the coast was fortified at Brownsea Island, between Hurst Castle to the east and Sandsfoot Castle and Portland Castle to the west. John Leland, the contemporary historian, wrote:

From the mouth of Poole Haven, upon the shore by the south-west, is, in a bay about 13 miles off, a fisher town called Sandwich and there is a pier and a little fresh water.

The oldest building in the parish of Swanage, with more medieval stonework than the Parish Church, stands below the Purbeck Hills at Godlingston. Here a fortified country house, Godlingston Manor, retains a remarkable rounded tower attached to the western end. This has stone walls five feet thick, apart from on the side attached to the rectangular house, and was built as a defensible refuge for use in times of trouble. Both the tower and the main south-facing frontage of the manor house date from c.1300.

Godlingston Manor in an Edwardian view, showing its frontage from the south-east, with the fortified tower to the left.

Victorian Countryside

Country view from the western end of the High Street, c.1890, looking north-east from east of Newton Manor, to Northbrook Road railway bridge (centre left) and the cemetery (further left).

Below: *Carrant's Court (left), on Court Hill, the birthplace of mason and contractor John Mowlem, seen from the south-west in the 1890s.*

Left: *The western end of Swanage town, sketched by Sir James Pelie 'from the road to Langton Matravers' on 28 August 1882.*

Victorian Countryside

Above: *The tiny duck pond opposite Carrant's Court, a stone trough known as the Lake, seen from the north-east, looking uphill towards the High Street, c.1890.*

The Swanage Brewery of Henry J. Panton and Co., in its penultimate state in the 1870s, standing on the north side of The Brook overlooking the site of Swanage Station.

Left: *Swanage Brewery in its final form (left), with an additional chimney (on its right), seen from The Brook when the permanent way for the railway was being laid in 1884.*

Victorian High Street

Above: *The Narrows, in the central section of the High Street, eastwards from Tatchell's boot store, in about 1895.*

Right: *Central section of the High Street, looking west from the Red Lion (far left) towards Spring Hill and Old Purbeck House (centre, top), painted by J.W.B. Gibbs in 1865.*

Brook footbridge and Drong alleyway, leading southwards up Spring Hill to Purbeck House, in a beautifully composed 'penny for them' pose of 1890.

Victorian High Street

Left: *The bend in the High Street east of Purbeck House, in a view looking west, with one of the decaying posters, beside the Drong, advertising a furniture sale before the building of the Town Hall in 1882.*

Right: *The eastern end of the High Street from Victoria Terrace (centre) to the Steam Packet Office and Royal Victoria Hotel (left), in a photograph that can be precisely dated to 14 February 1890 by the* Daily Telegraph *placard for the 'Parnell Commission' (vindicating Irish nationalist Charles Stewart Parnell).*

High Street shops looking downhill from Purbeck House and the Town Hall, in about 1900, with Parry Brothers advertising 'Tea Rose American lamp oil' next to butcher Frederick Vye (left) and facing T.S. Biggs & Co, wine-merchants, and Cross the tobacconist.

Victorian High Street

Above: *Leafy section of the Victorian High Street, west of the commercial area.*

Left: *Ladies, new-age Edwardian and very Victorian, beside the High Street shop of L. Hendon, 'greengrocer, fruiterer and florist', in 1901.*

Right: *The High Street at Spring Hill, topped by the tower of Purbeck House, looking northwards from The Brook in the vicinity of Swanage Station, c.1895.*

The home has walls three feet thick and may also have been fortified until the insertion of stone-mullioned windows in the 18th century and the addition of an 18th-century north-west wing. There is also a rebuilt cross-wing at the east end.

That it has survived at all is fortuitous. By 1867 it was derelict and threatened with demolition. Thomas Bond described its ramshackle state in a talk to the Purbeck Society:

I lament to add that these interesting remains have been permitted to fall into a sad state of dilapidation, and it is now contemplated to sweep them all away, to make room for a brand new farm-house, if for the require-ments of the agricultural magnates of the present day, who have wants unknown to the Purbeck gentry of times gone by. Such destruction will be deplored by every-one who has any regard for mediaeval architecture, or even for what is merely picturesque.

Damaged by fire in 1871, Godlingston survived against all the odds, and came into National Trust ownership when the charity inherited the 16 000 acres of the Corfe Castle and Kingston Lacy Estates on the death of Ralph Bankes in 1981. It is not open to visitors but two public footpaths pass the building from Washpond Lane.

The prize exhibit in the Tithe Barn Museum, a 17th-century building just east of St Mary's Church which was given to the town by Tony Parsons in 1976, is the Gibbet Stone, aka the Gallows Stone. This heavy, rough-hewn mortised boulder was removed from the top of Court Hill where it stood at the western end of the development line in the High Street until Victorian times. It is holed at the centre for a wooden shaft, from which an arm would have extended at the top to hold chains and an iron girdle or frame in which a body could be suspended – after being hanged elsewhere on a gallows.

Towards the end of the summer in 1685 the town would have received its gory share of the five victims of Judge Jeffreys' Bloody Assize at Dorchester who were hanged, drawn and quartered at Wareham. This was in the aftermath of the Duke of Monmouth's defeat at the Battle of Sedgemoor and portions of his supporters and their vanquished peasant army were distributed across the western counties to blacken and blister in the sun, as a warning to the populace of the grim price of revolutionary failure. At this time, the Hearth Tax Returns of 1664 reveal, 'Swanidge Tythinge' had 38 well-heeled homes with such luxuries as an open fire.

In the landscape, before the southern hills became pockmarked by quarrying, open strip fields stretched from Chapel Lane (then Derrick Lane) due south for a mile to the common grazing of the Town Ware above Anvil Point. 'Ware' or 'Weares' survives as a placename on Portland for clifftop pastures. All

the walls and access paths south of Swanage still run from north to south.

In the other direction, by post-medieval times, the parish boundary between Swanage and Studland was set in stone. A series of boundary stones runs along the parish line for more than a mile along the hog's back spine of Ballard Down. They can be found from the slopes of the Ulwell Gap in the west to the exposed chalk of Ballard Cliff in the east. From here the boundary drops seaward, towards Swanage, to yield Ballard Point (or Head) to Studland. On the top, the administrative boundary became a fence-line but traditionally it was un-hedged as an open sheep-leaze. National Trust ownership, on both sides, has secured the restoration of open grassland.

The main length of the summit, for 2050 yards, was marked in the 18th century by eight marker stones which were cut on the south-facing side with the letters 'SM' for Swanage Manor.

Swanage was then in the Anglican diocese of Bristol. In Bishop Secker's survey of 1735–37 it appears as 'Swanwich, alias Sandwich, alias Worth Sandwich'. The latter status dates back to the Saxon status of Swanage as a chapelry of Worth Matravers, sharing the same clergyman, which gave rise to the track between the two communities being known as the Priest's Way which has its junction with the High Street beside Parker's Stores, which has one of the most characterful stone roofs in town.

'The Rectory of Worth with Chapelry of Swanwich' was the description until 1486 when the future ascendancy came to pass. Henceforth the liaison featured Swanage first: 'The Rectory of Swanwich alias Worth.' Then, in 1506, the position was officially reversed to recognise the situation on the ground, with the ascendancy of Swanage. St Mary's, at Swanage, became the mother church, with a rector, and Worth had a vicarage, with clerical appointments there being made by the rector in Swanage.

In 1737, in Swanage, there was 'one poor widow and two children' who were Papists, and 50 Presbyterians from about 20 families. The parish had 190 Anglican families, 37 Presbyterian families, one family of Roman Catholics 'who go to Mass at Lulworth', but no Methodists.

In the town, towards the western end of the High Street, Newton Manor was the ancient seat of the Cockram family, from 1597. It has 17th-century walls hidden behind a castellated three-storey Georgian façade which was added by Thomas Cockram. Interior fittings include a wealth of carvings, a staircase with scrolled balusters, and frieze-work dated 1656 and 1658. These are later insertions, brought to the house during its occupancy by Sir Charles Robinson, who was art adviser to the Victoria and Albert Museum. After his death in 1913 it became Newton Manor School, until closure in 1980 and house building across its grounds.

Edwardian Seaside

The Edwardian seaside at New Swanage, with Sea Bank Lodge (far left) and Shore Villa, in a lively study by Swanage photographer Thomas Powell.

New Swanage and Edwardian users from Tom Shiner's Mixed Bathing tents to the Highcliffe Private Hotel and the Grand Hotel.

Edwardian Town

St Mary's Church and the former Mill Pond Farm, with the water dammed above it (bottom left), seen from the south-west in about 1905.

Cosy suburbia, looking northwards down Park Road, to New Swanage where Edwardian development was taking place.

One more art object has come its way. This is the fish weather-vane from Billingsgate Market which was purloined by Victorian contractor George Burt during rebuilding in 1850 and brought to his new Purbeck House in Swanage in 1875. It was removed to Newton Manor, as a precautionary measure, having almost blown off Purbeck House when the latter was empty after the Burt family left in 1920.

By the 1600s the High Street was the single narrow road through Swanage, wandering the mile from the shore to Herston, and it was choked with buildings, compared with the almost empty fields on either side. The huddles of cottages were amongst the most picturesque in Dorset, looking Cotswold-style with their stone roofs, and Cornish in their coastal setting. Most have gone, as photographs in this book prove, and the single surviving cluster of real character are those in the vicinity of St Mary's Parish Church and the Mill Pond. Yet even the latter is of historically recent date, having been created around a spring in 1754, and later enlarged.

Gentrified Swanage was initially represented by the Bullen family, who provided Nelson with a captain at Trafalgar, and made their home in Newton Cottage which is now known as Heather Close. This rather plain Georgian house, built in 1800, stands on the north side of the High Street to the east of Newton Manor and features with Godlingston Manor in Swanage ghost stories.

Swanwic House, in Kings Road West immediately north-east of St Mary's Church, is the former rectory. It is one of the oldest buildings in the town. There is what seems to be medieval masonry in the east wall. The north-east side of the older part of the house dates from the 17th century and has an inscription '1667 W. R. July 10th' for rector William Rose. Southwards, the symmetrical frontage has the plat-band, architraves and key-stone of a Georgian centrepiece, circa 1750. Further expansion took place a century later.

The first Swanage census, taken in 1801, records the town – still generally known as Swanwich – as having 300 households with a population of 1382. This compares with Wareham with 1627 people in 381 homes. Corfe Castle, at half the size of the towns on either side of it, had 741 inhabitants and 152 dwellings.

The typical Swanage cottage was small and low. Measuring the outside, it was 25 feet by 18 feet, with one large room on the ground floor. Rough stone slabs covered the floor which could be expected to be damp. There was a pantry on one side of the room and a large, open fireplace on the other, with an inglenook used for smoking bacon on the right and a brick-built oven to the left. To the right of the fireplace – the cooler side – a staircase, or just a ladder, led up to the upstairs which had a wattle-and-daub partition to convert it into two bedrooms. The ceiling was only at head height at the level section across the centre.

Towards the outer walls it would slope down to a far lower height.

Four such cottages stood on the site of the Town Hall which was built between 1881 and 1883. Here the ground fell away to The Brook and creek. Front bedroom windows were on a level with the High Street and people could be expected to look in as the dwellings projected three feet into the road. Between two of the cottages was a narrow passage called The Drong, this being the Dorset dialect word for an alleyway, and there was another 'drongway' a short distance downhill. Almost opposite, either side of L. Hendon's fruiterers, were three old cottages, including one with gable-end stonework which squeezed across the pavement and was used as the town's notice board. This remained one of the last rustic corners of the High Street until demolition in 1959.

Beer was made at Gillingham's Malthouse, overlooking Tilly Mead on the north side of what would be the Swanage Station site, from the time of the Napoleonic Wars. Later known as Panton's Brewery it was gutted by fire on 8 November 1854 and rebuilt by owner James Panton. *Kelly's Directory* of 1889 enthused:

The properties of the water here are considered as good as those of Burton-on-Trent, as analysed by Doctors Letheby and Graham, and is exclusively used by Messrs. Panton at their brewery, the produce of which has long been characteristically known as 'Swanage Pale Ale'.

Note that the water, by culvert from Springfield, was as good as that from Burton. Cynics used to say it was a pity that the same could not be said for the beer!

Late in the 18th century, when even Wareham could seem like foreign parts, an old soldier living in Swanage became Purbeck's first postman. Jos Rawles connected Swanage with the main mail network. Each Monday, Wednesday and Friday he walked from Swanage to Wareham, via Kingston and Corfe Castle, and went the other way on Tuesday, Thursday and Saturday. Mailbags were carried on each journey and he collected and delivered en route. He would handle 25 items on the average daily walk.

Jos Rawles carried a pair of loaded pistols slung at his side. Later the horse was an innovation for the postman of 1800 who could then travel to Wareham and back each day. William Masters would be the first driver of a mail cart, introduced in the 1820s, and did extra business by taking passengers. In 1848 the Purbeck mail still comprised only 30 or so items a day. Real advances, from the 1840s, followed establishment of the penny post and a mail coach then joined the service, leaving at 09.00 hours and returning from Wareham at 15.00 hours. A coach-and-four was then introduced, from the Red Lion at Wareham, with Wareham having become a railway town – therefore a post town – in 1847.

Thirties Swanage

Above: *Between the groynes on Swanage beach in the 1930s.*

Above and Left: *The beach at New Swanage in the 1930s and Beach Road, now Shore Road, looking southwards.*

Elizabethan Times

Left: *The Mowlem Institute, built on the seafront in 1863 by John Mowlem, and seen advertising* Ruddigore *before demolition in 1966 and replacement by the Mowlem Theatre and Restaurant.*

Right: *Herston House, main home of the Mowlem family in mid-Victorian times, before demolition in 1967.*

Below: *Swanage beach looking northwards to the Grand Hotel (top left) and the chalk cliffs of Ballard Down, in a time-warp shot by Colin Graham in July 1985.*

Elizabethan Times

Once typical but now rare, Olive Cottage stands beside a stepped Cliff Place and has three small front rooms, one on top of the other.

The Gibbet Stone, from which bodies were hanged in chains, found beside the road into town and now displayed at the museum.

The Tithe Barn Museum, with an ammonite in its wall and cannon-bollards beside the forecourt, facing the Parish Church.

Elizabethan Times

*The stone quay apparently timeless and peaceful in about 1950,
but there is a warship in the bay (glimpsed off Ballard Point).*

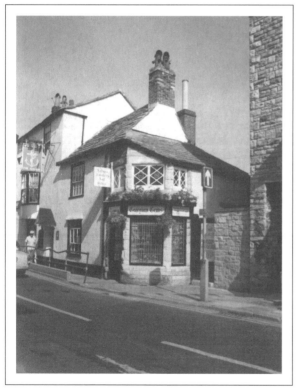

*Georgian Gems, tucked into a corner beside the
Anchor Hotel, has been a jewellers since 1929
and claims to be the smallest shop in England.*

*The Parade, on the site of the stone bankers
in Institute Road, facing a lively sea.*

Seaside Swanage, in the sense that we know it, has its beginnings in Marine Villas on the Pier approach at the eastern end of the High Street. There was originally a single Marine Villa which was built by William Morton Pitt MP as his coastal summer house in 1825. Stucco rendered and embellished with attractive wrought-iron trelliswork porches, this Regency building was erected purely for pleasure – with baths, billiard room and coffee room – and was the setting for entertaining the Duke of Gloucester and a party of well-heeled yachtsmen who arrived from Lulworth Cove during their stay at Lulworth Castle in 1828.

Pitt had lost his great houses at Kingston Maurward and Encombe through a series of philanthropic enterprises to provide work for artisans and the rural poor. One such business had been a fish-curing plant at Swanage. He was the first person to show faith in the potential of Swanage as a seaside spa. He used his final tranche of inherited wealth to acquire the Manor House, which had been built in about 1724 by stone merchant John Chapman (1681–1735), on land acquired from Sir William Phippard MP, and was also known as the Great House.

It faced seawards from the eastern end of the High Street and would be transformed by Pitt into the Swanage Hotel, which became the Royal Victoria Hotel before his death in 1836. He also rebuilt the stone quay and provided the Coast Guard service with a Preventive Station on Peveril Point. Swanage had been transformed but he and Mrs Pitt had 'beggared' themselves in the process.

'God Almighty has spared my life to improve the place where I first drew breath,' quarry owner and contractor John Mowlem confided to his diary in 1848, but anything he could do a nephew would achieve on a scale 100 times bigger. The next power-house of Swanage would be at the centre of the High Street. There a large Georgian building was destined to become Purbeck House, being bought by civil engineer George Burt, and rebuilt in Victorian gothic in 1875. The *Land Agents' Record* of 6 June 1891 was in no doubt that Burt was emphatically the 'Father' of Swanage. "Why?" said one we interrogated with a knowing twinkle in his eye, "old Burt has brought half London down to Swanage".

Purbeck House (left of centre) before rebuilding in 1874, with its summer house beside Sunshine Walk (behind, left) and the southern skyline, pock-marked by quarrying.

Purbeck House as rebuilt by George Burt, and now Purbeck House Hotel, seen from its lawn to the south.

Designed by Weymouth architect George Crickmay, in what has been aptly dubbed 'Scottish Baronial', the rebuilt Purbeck House is a rusticated extravaganza of secondhand taste with London writ large. The cylindrical granite bollard in the stable-yard entrance is from Millbank Penitentiary. Ditto, probably, the pair of granite gate-piers. There is an archway from the Duke of Westminster's Grosvenor Place home; two 15th-century windows; historic iron columns; and three statues dating from the 17th century. Of the latter, one came from Billingsgate Market, and the other two were from the ruins of the Royal Exchange which was burnt out in 1836. They are royal figures representing, probably, Henry V and Edward I.

Fragments of moulded stone and floor tiles came from the lobbies of the Houses of Parliament during the rebuilding of the Palace of Westminster. They include a mosaic with the Prince of Wales' motto and feathers emblem, with a red background, in a hexagonal surround. 'The King of Swanage,' as Thomas Hardy called him, went on to create a landscape to match, all the way to Durlston Head and Tilly Whim Caves. The approach roads were marketed to an admiring public as sites for 'Marine Residences in this favourite Seaside Resort' with 88 plots being auctioned by Baker and Son of London in a marquee on the Durlston Park Estate, on 29 June 1891. These were in Park Road, Durlston Road, Bon Accord Road, Purbeck Terrace Road, Durlston Crescent, and south of The Shrubbery.

Purbeck House would be vacated by the Burt and Mowlem families in 1920 and remained empty for many years, offers of its freehold being declined by Swanage Urban District Council, before becoming the Convent of the Sisters of Mercy in 1935. It is now Purbeck House Hotel.

Swanage Post Office moved to its purpose-built premises near the railway station, from the High Street, in 1908. Edwardian Swanage had 16 postal workers, handling a volume of letters and parcels that totalled 21 294 items in the 'count' of a sample week.

The best restaurant in Swanage between the two world wars was the Trocadero – the fashionable 'Troc' - at the south end of The Parade in Lower High Street where Edwardian shops and flats had been erected on the site of the former quarry-stone bankers, in 1905. The Troc specialised in crab and lobster salads and cream teas.

The *Swanage Times*, the local newspaper, was founded in 1821 and became a slip-edition of the *Dorset County Chronicle* from 1830 to 1940. It then went through several transformations, first with new owner Eric Putnam in the 1950s, and then merger with the *Poole Herald* in the 1960s, though still preserving its identity with its own front and back pages. Times-Herald Newspapers became the *Advertiser* series of free newspapers in the 1980s which maintain the tradition of a Swanage edition.

Panoramic view of Swanage Bay, by Colin Graham in 1985, overlooking St Mary's Church tower (bottom, left) and Swanage Station (right), across two miles of water to Ballard Down and Ballard Point.

Chapter 3
WESLEY AND VICTORIA

*Wesley's Cottage in the High Street, where the preacher stayed
in 1774, would be destroyed by a German bomb in 1941.*

Figuratively, two eminent visitors put Swanage on the map, either side of its debut on the real thing which was in 1811 with the first edition of the Ordnance Survey. The founder of Methodism, England's rural religion, came in October 1774 and was followed by the leading lady of the British Empire in August 1833. John Wesley (1703–91) and Princess Victoria (1819–1901) made waves that still have their ripples.

Wesley would make three visits to the Isle of Purbeck and the first was by direct request. Mary Burt heard that he was in Salisbury and set off walking to fetch him. She had her baby in her arms. The distance would have been about 45 miles. A rather ambiguous footnote in the 71-year-old preacher's journal records that he acceded to the invitation, and arrived with the lady in his carriage (though perhaps she was still following on foot). The church historian writes: 'No doubt Mrs Burt and her baby returned with Wesley in the chaise.'

There was no declared Wesleyan community in Swanage but two female friends, from the Collins and Webber families, may have gone with her. The church records get off to a hesitant start. What seems certain is that John Wesley spent Wednesday 12 October 1774 in Purbeck and addressed three open-air meetings. The first was to a large congregation at Corfe Castle, literally at the crack of dawn – 05.00 hours – followed by a big and serious Puritan-minded gathering at Langton Matravers at noon. He arrived in Swanage, to a larger congregation in a meadow, in the evening where the hymn-writer was introduced to the crowd as 'the sweet singer of the new Israel'. Of this audience, 'three or four persons, all of one family, seemed really to enjoy the faith of the gospel.' Others of the society, 'between thirty and forty in number', did not appear to have been convinced by his message of sin. Wesley expressed disappointment that his preaching was falling on stony ground.

He then went on to spend the night at Mary Burt's cottage, next to the Town Hall, about 50 yards away from the present Methodist Church, on the opposite side of the High Street. It would be henceforth known as Wesley's Cottage until it was damaged and demolished after being hit by a German bomb on 14 May 1941. Its name-stone survived and has been re-set near the site.

Wesley would return to Purbeck, to Corfe Castle, on Thursday 5 September 1776. His third and final visit would be to Swanage on Monday 13 August 1787, completely unscheduled and unannounced, as a result of a south-westerly gale which caused the ship which was taking him to Guernsey to take shelter in Swanage Bay. Providence reintroduced him to the little Wesleyan society:

I had not seen them for 13 years and had no thought of seeing them now; but God does all things well. In the evening I preached in the Presbyterian meeting house – not often, I believe, so well filled; and afterwards passed half an hour very agreeably with the minister in the parsonage house, which he rents, a neat retired house, with a delightful garden. Thence we adjourned to the house of our old brother Collins and between eight and nine [o'clock] went on board.

Revd William Sedcole was the Presbyterian minister and he rented the Anglican parsonage from the rector, Revd Richard Williams, who was a bachelor and had taken lodgings. Ken Faulkner showed me the position of the Presbyterian Meeting House, which had been built in 1705, on the site of the hall adjoining the present United Reform Church. He pointed out that the Meeting House was second only to the Parish Church in being the oldest religious building in Swanage. Lacking their own chapel, the Wesleyans met in a room up a flight of steps beside No. 8 Purbeck Place (99 High Street). Swanage historian and builder William Masters Hardy described it much as a building inspector would. He gives the dimensions as 14 feet by 12 feet with a beam across the middle about 4 feet 6 inches above the floor, so that those moving across the room had to bend below it. The roof also sloped in on both sides, reducing the ceiling to a strip 5 feet wide in the centre and 6 feet 6 inches high. There was a single old lea-light window, about 4 feet by 3 feet, in the gabled southern end.

John Wesley was shown into the little room but declared it was too small for a meeting. They therefore asked to use the Presbyterian Meeting House. Aspirations for something better followed a period of growth in their numbers, from 26 in 1799 to 40 in 1804, coupled with an increasingly comfortable commercial status as the Napoleonic Wars brought activity and money to the coast. Nonconformists tended to run the stone trade which in both Purbeck and Portland had developed a long tradition of independent customs. They were in tune with free-thought being brought to religious practices. Samuel Wesley, the father of John and Charles Wesley, was Dorset-born – at Winterborne Whitechurch – and had gone to school in Dorchester. John Westleigh, the rector of Langton Matravers in 1481, may have been an ancestor.

Wesley's adherents petitioned Dorset Quarter Sessions in Dorchester, at the Epiphany term in 1808, for a Dissenters' Certificate in respect of their first Methodist Church which had been built beside the High Street in Swanage at a cost of £980 and had 250 sittings. The petition was signed by Jonathan Burt, Timothy Burt, Thomas Coleman, Thomas Hardy, John Phippard and John Thicks. Their request was granted:

At this Court was brought a certificate that a certain building situate in the Parish of Swanage in the County of Dorset is intended to be set apart for the Public Worship of Almighty God by a congregation of Dissenting Protestants called Methodists and it was desired that the Court would enter and file the same of record. This Court doth therefore record the same and the same is entered and recorded accordingly.

By 1820, Ken Faulkner's records show that the Swanage Society had 59 members, including original stalwart Mary Burt, with other well-known Purbeck family names being Bower, Collins, Hardy, Haysom, Manwell, Melmoth and Stickland. The numbers fluctuated for a while and then increased to 83, in a parish of 1900 souls, in time for the accession of Queen Victoria on 20 June 1837.

She was a Swanage lass, by adoption, as a result of just two days in 1833 which left memories which lasted as long as her reign. She had outlived just about all of her original subjects when she died in 1901. The previous personage of importance to visit the town had been the Duke of Gloucester, sailing round from Lulworth Cove in 1828, but Princess Victoria – as we now say – was something else. Her visit turned the Swanage Hotel into the Royal Victoria Hotel and forced the rector, Revd Thomas Oldfeld Bartlett, to rise from his sick-bed.

His diary, transcribed by Richard Bartelot, shows that he was 'very poorly the whole day' on Sunday 4 August 1833 when he delivered his text from Ezekiel (chapter 14, verse 20) in the morning, and Luke (chapter 4, verse 23) in the afternoon. He had publicly christened Mary Jane Stephen and Alan Martin and in the evening privately baptised James Tollifield, the first son of Jane and James Tollifield. 'Violent spasms in my back and chest' followed on the Monday, but he was feeling rather better when he heard that he was about to host a royal visit:

News came this afternoon that the Duchess of Kent and her daughter the Princess Victoria would sleep at Swanage Hotel [next] Wednesday night and proceed to Norris Castle, Isle of Wight, in the Emerald *yacht, towed by one of His Majesty's steamers the next day.*

It promised to be the biggest day in Swanage life of that century and the next, and would not be eclipsed until King George VI arrived to the sound of the guns and the whole town rocked to the concussive thud of war on 18 April 1944.

In 1833, Princess Victoria was the heir-presumptive. 'I am nearer the throne than I thought,' Drina (her family name, being a contraction of her first name, Alexandrina) remarked to her governess. 'So it is, Madam,' she replied, though others pointed out that she 'might even at the eleventh hour be stayed at the very steps to the throne by the good King's posthumous issue'. The Duchess of Kent was sure there would be no shock from beyond the grave and that her daughter would succeed William IV. She had arranged their pilgrimage to the shrine of the 'Dairyman's Daughter' in Arreton, as well as the visits in the *Emerald* 'over the bright and merry waters of the Channel to several of the principal places of the southern coast.'

Thus Swanage would be mentioned in the same breath as Plymouth, Torquay and Southampton. The arrivals were carefully choreographed and orchestrated, with local dignitaries competing to give loyal addresses of welcome, as bands played and troops paraded, to the rousing accompaniment of 'enthusiastic acclamations of the populace'.

The Dorset party preparing to dine with the Duchess of Kent and Princess Victoria at Swanwich Hotel (its official name) included John Hales Calcraft MP and his wife Lady Caroline Calcraft, daughter of the Earl of Manchester, of Rempstone Hall, Corfe Castle; Lady Caroline Morant, a sister of Lord Errol, the Master of the Horse; Lady Isabella St John, a daughter of the Duke and Duchess of Grafton; and Mr and Mrs Dawson Damer of Came House, Dorchester, who were members of the family of the Marquess of Hertford.

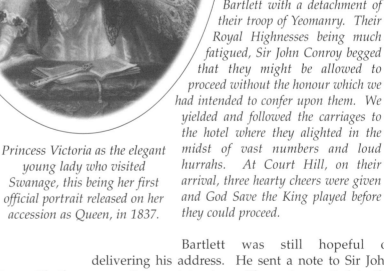

Princess Victoria as the elegant young lady who visited Swanage, this being her first official portrait released on her accession as Queen, in 1837.

Thomas Oldfeld Bartlett threw himself into making sure that the reception they received in Swanage would pass muster. By 09.00 hours on Wednesday 7 August he had held a meeting to rehearse his welcoming address. An hour later he was waiting to receive Sir John Conroy, the Duchess of Kent's aide-de-camp, for his approval of the plans. A further town meeting followed at which it was agreed that the rector:

... with the churchwardens, principal inhabitants and the two clubs with their banners and the band, should at five o'clock be at Court Hill, and await the arrival of the party.

They would then lead the royal group to the Swanage Hotel. Bartlett's reception committee would be kept waiting on Court Hill for three and a half hours before a rider came at full speed crying out: 'They are coming! They are coming!' The rector takes up the story:

All was instantly in order and upon the royal carriages coming to us they stopped and were greeted by Captain M. Bond, Lieutenant Fyler, and Cornet Charles Oldfeld Bartlett with a detachment of their troop of Yeomanry. Their Royal Highnesses being much fatigued, Sir John Conroy begged that they might be allowed to proceed without the honour which we had intended to confer upon them. We yielded and followed the carriages to the hotel where they alighted in the midst of vast numbers and loud hurrahs. At Court Hill, on their arrival, three hearty cheers were given and God Save the King played before they could proceed.

Bartlett was still hopeful of delivering his address. He sent a note to Sir John requesting an interview. The rector waited in the passage of the hotel with his brother – 'in full regimentals' – standing at his side. Sir John listened to the address 'in the kindest way' and took the copy of it to the Duchess. He then returned to say that she would receive it at 10.30 hours in the morning. Charles walked with Thomas back to the rectory. The detachment of Yeomanry mounted up in half an hour and returned to Wareham. By 23.00 hours, the rector was making his final copy of the address, and 'went to bed completely tired, but much gratified'.

On Thursday 8 August, at 10.00 hours, Thomas Oldfeld Bartlett advanced in his gown, 'with the churchwardens and many respectable inhabitants', to the Swanage Hotel on the seafront. He resumes his account:

Had an interview with Sir John Conroy and said that Mrs Bartlett and my eldest daughter were in waiting, humbly hoping that the Duchess would permit the former to present an address and the latter a straw bonnet of the finest plait of the place to Princess Victoria. Soon got an answer that they were much pleased and would be most happy to receive both. Now petitioned that the ladies may be permitted to enter the great room and see all. Granted, and Sir John requested me to arrange the ladies on either side of the room leaving the middle quite free for their Royal Highnesses to enter, the gentlemen all remaining in the passages, and I at the door awaiting the arrival of the Duchess and her daughter at the time appointed. They entered smiling and curtseying kindly to me, and then advanced to the head of the room. Then I advanced bowing (the gents following and doing the same), till I came close to her Royal Highness and the amicable Princess, when they both curtsied and smiled most graciously to me.

The rector welcomed them: 'Ma'am, I am deputed by the principal inhabitants to congratulate your Royal Highness on your arrival here.' He then read the address:

May it please your Royal Highness. We, the Rector, Churchwardens, and principal inhabitants of the town of Swanage humbly approach your Royal Highness to offer our most respectful congratulations on the arrival of your Royal Highness and your Illustrious Daughter to this place. We feel highly honoured at this condescending visit of Royalty, the first perhaps, ever paid to our retired little town – and we beg now to assure you of our loyalty and attachment to the House of Brunswick. We sincerely pray that lengthened life, health, and every blessing may be allotted to both your Royal Highness and your Illustrious Daughter – to whom we look forward (though we trust at a distant period) as the future ruler of this nation, and who, we have reason to believe, by her present amiable disposition (following the advice and example given her by your Royal Highness) must win the love and affection of a grateful people.

He confided in his journal: 'My friends flatter me and say I did it very well, and her Royal Highness made a most delightful reply.'

It was then the turn of Mrs Elizabeth Bartlett and 12-year-old Mary Frances Vincent Bartlett to be introduced by Sir John Conroy, with the rector's wife presenting her address and the daughter the Swanage-made bonnet, production of which was a local speciality. The Duchess and Princess said they would order bonnets and suggested the maker, Mrs Shorey, used the Princess' arms and name as Bonnet Maker to Her Royal Highness. The Duchess then said how very much they were 'gratified by this kind reception' and gave the rector a personal goodbye: 'Oh, Sir, I thank you for all your kindness.'

They then 'almost instantly embarked' at the nearby quay, 'amidst loud cheers of immense numbers and the band playing'. It was 11.00 hours as the *Emerald* was towed up-Channel, over the horizon into the Solent, and around to Norris Castle on the headland opposite Cowes. This was 'Dear Norris' in the grounds of which, in 1845, Queen Victoria and husband Albert would build Osborne House. As for the busiest-ever Swanage morning the *Dorset County Chronicle* concluded: 'The weather was delightful, and the scene altogether such as we have never witnessed before, but heartily desire to see repeated.'

The next social event for an exuberant Bartlett family was dinner at the rectory. The rector's father, Captain Thomas Bartlett of Holwell Manor and Wareham, had raised a troop of horsemen against Napoleonic invasion and been made Barrack Master of Great Britain, in 1804. He would die in 1836 at the age of 81, and the rector would follow him in 1841, at the age of 52. Four-year-old Elizabeth Burton Leach Bartlett, representing the new generation, would reach the age of 96 in 1925. Like most of the family she would marry inside the clergy (the males doing likewise with daughters of clergymen) and did her part to expand the ecclesiastical dynasty, through her union with Revd Henry Weare Blandford of Weston Bampfylde, Somerset, in 1861.

Concerning the more famous instance of longevity, the *Emerald* voyage nearly stopped the longest reign on record, before it had even started. For the yacht was in collision with the *Active* hulk, while heading from Eddystone to the Isle of Wight, and its mainmast was sprung, causing the top-mast to drop towards the very spot on the deck where Victoria was standing:

Fortunately the pilot, Mr Saunders, was regarding the Princess at the moment of the collision, and, seeing her danger, sprang towards her with admirable presence of mind, and, taking her in his arms, saved her from sudden death.

As for the Swanage Hotel, it announced itself as the 'Royal Victoria Hotel, Swanwich, County of Dorset' in an advertisement at the top of the front page of the *Dorset County Chronicle* on 24 April 1834:

Miss Hardy begs to acquaint those who have hitherto bestowed upon her the honour of their approbation, as also the public in general, that various further improvements have been introduced into that Hotel lately, in addition to that important object, the Warm Air Apparatus, so beneficial to Invalids through the Winter. The Baths within the House, in particular, are now arranged on a new principle, not only extremely convenient to Residents in the Hotel, desirous of bathing shortly before they retire to rest, or at any other hour of the day, on the shortest notice, but also to others visiting Swanwich generally. The Baths are six in number, namely four warm and one cold sea Baths and one shower Bath, with Fire–places adjoining: Also a steam Bath, Douche, and Slipper Bath, conveyable to any Bed Chamber. The Hotel is likewise provided with a Bath Chair, a Sedan Chair, a Wheeling Sopha, and various other conveniences for the advantage of Invalids.

As with names in modern times, including my own father's Edward George (for the first 20th-century King and heir), Swanage honoured at least one of its daughters with the royal forenames. Richard Bartelot, researching the impact of the Swanage visitation, rounded off his story with Thomas Oldfeld Bartlett's baptism, in 1835, of Alexandrina Victoria Salter. Within two years her namesake would be Queen of England and later Empress of India.

In Swanage in accession year the town scandal was that John Toop had run out on his wife, Margaret, and left her depending on parish funds. The magistrates issued a warrant against him and the town recovered a total of £15.19s.4d.

Left: *Royal Victoria Hotel as depicted in its first woodcut advertisement.*

Below: *Today, converted into flats, it remains an imposing building.*

The view from the Victoria Hotel – before it was 'Royal' – as Princess Victoria saw it, looking towards Marine Villa, painted by C.M. Colvile.

Brian Brown

Princess Victoria's departure from the stone quay in front of the (Royal) Victoria Hotel was before the advent of photography but the town would gather there again, in sadness, for the funeral in September 1963 of fisherman Brian Brown who drowned while trying to secure a friend's boat in a gale.

Chapter 4
PRINCES AND KINGS

*Edward on returning to Dorset as King Edward
VII, for a social visit to Crichel in 1906.*

The formal education of Prince Edward (1841–1910), Queen Victoria's eldest son and heir, the future King Edward VII, included strenuous character-forming walking tours. The first of these which he set out on, in 1856 at the age of 15, started from Osborne House on the Isle of Wight and headed westwards through Dorset and Devon. Bertie, as he was known to family and familiars, set off towards the end of September and travelled incognito with two male aides. One was in his thirties and the other middle aged. Their perambulation of Dorset began at Sandbanks, from where they were ferried to Brownsea Island, and they then walked inland to visit Wimborne Minster. On 26 September they arrived in Swanage and booked into the Royal Victoria Hotel for the night. The landlord said he could only accommodate the two men: 'The young gentleman must put up with a sofa in the corridor.'

A suitable word in the man's ear avoided that fate but from here on the disguise was compromised and a fever of excitement and expectancy gripped the countryside. Though they set off from Swanage along the cliff path, following the Coastguard marker stones and passing the working quarries at Dancing Ledge, Hedbury, Seacombe and Winspit, the healthy exercise bit the dust on St Alban's Head. A carriage was waiting beside the Norman chapel on the clifftop. Stops followed at Wareham and Dorchester. Prince Edward was recognised as he attended a service in St Peter's Church in the heart of the county town. Popular interest erupted into the streets and became what today's tabloids would term 'Bertie mania' in the East Devon town of Honiton. The tour had to be abandoned.

As for Swanage, its next unscripted royal visit would come out of the air, at 13.15 hours during the wet and windy afternoon of 12 July 1933. Edward, the Prince of Wales (1894–1972), who would briefly reign as King Edward VIII, had flown in a de Havilland Moth from Hendon and passed over Bournemouth on a south-westerly course, heading into Dorset. He was due to open Weymouth Harbour and pier reconstruction.

Instead the Prince and his pilot met the weather head-on, as a gale lashed its way up the Channel, with the small aircraft being increasingly bumped and bounced by turbulence. Visibility also deteriorated as they attempted to follow the confusingly indented Purbeck coast. They had fleeting glimpses of an apparently moving shore-line – first north and then south and even to the east – as Poole Harbour became Studland Bay. 'Get down while we can still see something!' Prince Edward told his pilot, Flight-Lieutenant G.H. Fielden, as the Purbeck Hills added an alarming extra dimension to the problem. They reconnoitred the ground and decided upon a suitable field – in a comparatively level landscape below the ridge at Godlingston – by establishing its position in relation to the closest landmark. This was the chimney stack of the Swanage Brick and Tile Works. The aeroplane circled it a couple of times as they descended.

'We thought at first he was going to knock it off,' said works director B.P. Codling, in a reference to the chimney, 'but the plane came down nicely in a little wheat-field on the other side of the road from here.'

He identified the spot on the edge of the Bankes Estate which would pass into National Trust ownership in 1982. 'The pilot pulled her up by the side of a rick,' Mr Codling continued, noting:

Afterwards we could find no trace of its descent, the wheat being quite undamaged. Several of our tilers who were near rushed to the assistance of the plane, having seen it in the air, and got the impression it was in difficulties.

The pilot admitted to them that the landing had been far from easy. As for Prince Edward, he was given a lift to Weymouth, courtesy Captain F.R. Bacon from the brickworks. Britain and Europe's most fashionable dapper dresser arrived looking uncharacteristically none too spruce. He apologised to officials but insisted on proceeding with his ceremonial duties without further delay. 'His hair was very ruffled and his suede shoes were clogged with mud,' the *Dorset Daily Echo* reported. 'His trouser ends were bespattered with mud.'

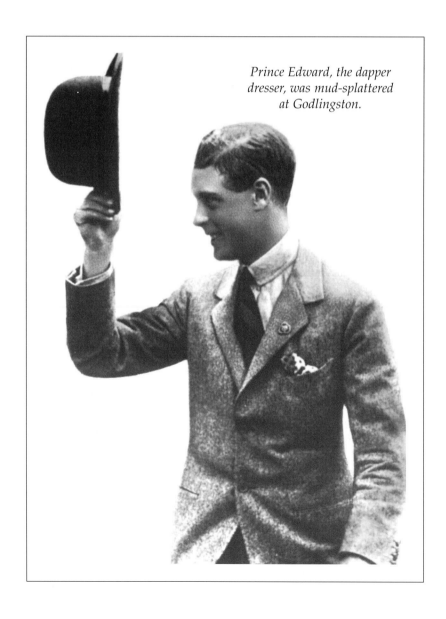

Prince Edward, the dapper dresser, was mud-splattered at Godlingston.

Chapter 5

QUARRIES AND QUARRYING

The famous Purbeck marble of the nation's cathedrals and effigies was worked further west and sledged to Corfe Castle for export from Ower Quay on Poole Harbour. Swanage's part in the 'chipping and shipping of stone,' as Charles Robinson called it in 1882, came in the trade's post-medieval revival. The greatest stone quarry in the whole of the Isle of Purbeck was where you would today least expect to find one. Overlooking the heart of Purbeck's holiday town, strung out above the High Street in a line for nearly a mile from Bon Accord Road westward to Belle Vue Farm at Herston are the vast disused workings of Swanage Townsend.

This was where stone lay conveniently close to cottages and the coast. It became the most intensively quarried part of all Purbeck and operated continuously from before 1700 to 1939 when Dowland's Quarry, overlooking Cowlease, was the last working. The creamish-yellow stone from this broad hillside has long ago weathered to the familiar grey of Purbeck buildings, sometimes with a tinge of pink. It is one of the best known British building stones.

A quarry is normally an open pit, but here was something quite different, with Cowlease being a full-scale stone mine with arms reaching 120 feet into the rock. These were the lanes and many were sunk into those two centuries of use. Each lane started with a slide – a steeply inclined shaft – and was a production line with carts taking fine limestone from passages that branched at various levels to the working faces on the roach, thornback, cinder (a bed of fossil oysters), downs-vein, caps and new-vein. Each deposit of clay or loose material parting the stone beds was known as a shiver or just plain dirt.

One of the Cowlease quarries, seen from the south-west with
Edwardian Swanage advancing up the slope towards the workings.

The 'quarr houses' of Cluny Quarry, before it became Cluny Crescent, in a view northwards taken in the 1860s, when Shore Villa was the only building in the northern curve of Swanage Bay.

The remains of at least 20 abandoned shafts can been seen in other parts of the 300 acres of the Townsend quarries. This method of working started about 1700. It was adapted in the year 1800 after William Coombs, a blacksmith at Court Hill, Swanage, made a chain cable. He was soon being asked by quarrymen to make more. Cables were found to be far stronger than rope.

The mine shafts were called 'slides' because they originally went into the ground at a low angle and were worked with carts without wheels that were simple sledges. With the introduction of cables the mine shafts became steeper. Though it caused draughts, the passages from two quarry lanes would occasionally connect together, making it possible to go down one shaft and surface at another hole. Underground, the ceiling was often only three feet high, though six feet was the ideal working height, and conditions were always clayey and damp. Good, hard stone had to be built up in pillars to hold the quarry roof. Had a section of strata simply been left it would have crumbled under the weight and given way. With seams being worked at several levels, these 'legs' had to be solid and strong to prevent 'founders', as collapses were called.

There were, however, times when pieces of Swanage fell through a quarry roof. John T. Dean explained that the only truly safe untouched island of land to the south of the High Street is the Cottage Hospital, on ground which the Burt family gave to the town. Elsewhere, he said, all the land is literally undermined:

It is still possible to lose a walking stick whilst walking up there – it just falls down almost anywhere, out of sight. My great-uncle Tom grazed his baker's horse there for years. One Sunday just after the Great War, he was actually watching it, when it dropped out of sight where it stood. It went down 25 feet, its hind quarters stuck, and despite ten men digging had to be shot five hours later. Certainly entire houses will drop up there, such as the twin house Sentryfields, at the top of Seymer Road, which although identical in size, disappeared entirely just before the Great War. It is not the weight of the houses; it is all on the move anyway.

In about 1895 the western house of Alexandra Terrace collapsed into an eastern lane from the Cowlease. But, generally, the workmanship of the old men is still standing surprisingly well and the quarry legs, even as they powder, hold parts of residential Swanage proudly in the sunlight. The spreading Townsend housing estate has covered the lower edge of the quarrylands and elsewhere it is blackthorn and brambles that obscure the openings to the slides. Ivy smothers the ruins of old work huts and everywhere there are the heaps of overburden and 'spawls'. Piles of stone waste were also known as 'scar-heaps'.

These mounds and craters cover the entire hillside rising above the southern side Swanage. The larger hillocks merge beside continuous surface workings. Even from the top of the ridge you can look across to further pits beyond California Farm. Westwards into the parish of Langton Matravers – either side of the Priest's Way and the seemingly normal fields beyond the Swanage parish boundary at Verney Farm, to South Barn, and along the track beside Leeson Park – most of this slope is undermined. The openings of some 15 shafts are still visible.

In the other direction, above the High Street from Chapel Lane to Bell Street, the town's tentacles of bungalow development have moved up the hill, but a wasteland lies above. Because of the danger from the old workings caving in, planning permission has been consistently refused for building further up the hillside. This has been to the town's advantage, as a natural, if pockmarked, skyline can be seen to the south of Swanage and it is better to look up at a green hill than watch buildings clamber over to the next obstacle. The view in reverse, from any part of the slopes, overlooks the entire Swanage valley with the town distended from right to left, strung out along the High Street from the shore to Herston. Here Pat Henshaw discovered a narrow-gauge mineral railway in the form of 'a short rope-worked incline' used to take stone 'from a group of quarries to a sawmill'.

It is hard to visualise this as the heart of a great industry. All the workings are abandoned and the grass-grown spoil heaps that heave everywhere seem tossed imperceptibly together. Each dip is filled with dense clumps of thorn, bramble and elder. All the shafts have been partially or completely filled and the biggest hole remaining in the early 1970s was a few yards from the bungalows, a short distance south-east of the end of Hillside Road and just east of the old stone wall that is now the boundary of Swanage Urban Council's caravan site. The nearby Grandfather's Knap is the biggest of the spawl heaps, having accumulated from six quarries over 40 years.

In *Purbeck Island*, in 1972, I described this area of industrial archaeology and called for its preservation:

This shaft is 30 feet wide and 20 feet deep with three sheer sides of the natural rock reinforced with drystone walling; a pit in which the body of a discarded car looks quite small. From the fourth side, the north, a wide and steep shaft rises from the bottom. A few feet northward from its head stands a perfectly preserved capstan with its stones complete but the wooden parts, as would be expected, have rotted away. Around these historic stones, and hiding them from attention, is a thick clump of bushes. It was only after two days of searching, and when winter had lessened the screen, that I found this relic. A century ago, chains from its horse-operated hub were raising stone by the ton, but

Disused Tomes family stone mine east of Belle Vue Farm, photographed from outside its 'quarr houses' by Colin Graham, with inside shots by Rodney Legg showing its crabstones, the 'slide' half-way down, and the underground working floor.

it is now the best remaining capstan in Purbeck. Nearby are the walls of quarry sheds, called quarr houses, and the two crabstones that supported a smaller capstan drum. All this, however, is little enough to see on the actual site of a great industry and Swanage Council should be encouraged to preserve the Cowlease and its antiquities as a public open space.

The Townsend Quarries, I added, were facing a future of quick change. Some of the area had been re-dug by open pits, other parts were being levelled, and another concealed a caravan camp. I phoned several Swanage councillors and followed this up in *Dorset: The County Magazine:*

The last historic relics of underground working in the Purbeck stone trade lie alarmingly close to new housing estates in the old quarrylands above the High Street at Swanage. Industrial archaeologists will have to act immediately to save them for the future. Only two pairs of crabstones survive; these once held wooden capstans to haul carts of stone up from the mine shafts. Donkeys walked around the crabstones in a circular towpath, pulling a lever to turn the capstan. Jeffery Curtis, who is now in Blackpool, lived in Alexandra Terrace, opposite the quarries on Cowlease Hill, until 1942.

He recalled for me one of the crabstone pairs still working Bower's Quarry in 1939:

I can remember clearly because his donkey was stung by an adder on its face. The quarry just kept on working, it was the last one left above Swanage, but then it suddenly closed. Today, you can still faintly follow round the circle where the donkey used to walk.

Mr Curtis came from a quarrying family and his uncle Ron, and Eric and Fred Bower had a modern open-pit working above Worth Matravers on the Acton Road.

As an occasional visitor to Purbeck, Mr Curtis warned that these capstan supports – 'they are the last two left apart from a couple stuck in a wall on Priest's Road' – were perilously close to the spreading development:

I reckon the Council should take them out and put them in a place where they can be mounted again with a dummy capstan in the middle to show people what they were used for. The quarries themselves will go as all the quarr houses are gone and the shafts have been filled in. These crabstones are all that's left of a whole industry that's been going on in Purbeck since the Romans.

There was agreement from David Haysom of Alexandra Terrace:

I was most interested to read in Dorset Magazine *the account given by Mr Curtis of the last remaining crabstones that once served the stone industry of Cowlease at Swanage. The ones referred to as being at Mr Bower's quarry are actually standing in the quarry once worked by Mr C. Benfield more than 50 years ago. This quarry was last worked by Mr C. Dowland from another shaft facing west, in the same quarry.*

The crabstones at Mr F. Bower's quarry are partially destroyed and can still be seen above the two shafts. They also worked two slides from one quarry, one going south-west and the other north-west under the new Hoburne Road. Two other pairs of crabstones can also be seen with 150 yards of the previously mentioned quarries, one pair once used by Mr Squibb and later by Mr W. Brown and Mr Chinchen, the other pair standing within 30 yards of Manwell Estate and last used by Mr Joe Norman.

In Cowlease alone approximately 37 positions of shafts can be traced to this day, Cowlease being the most quarried area in Purbeck. Incidentally, with reference to your mention of Cowlease, I have what I am sure is the only model of this quarry in existence. It stands in my garden.

David Haysom wrote a further letter to *Dorset: The County Magazine*, in 1978, recording the destruction of most of the Cowlease workings and pleading for the preservation of the remainder:

During the past twelve months the majority of the remaining workings have been completely obliterated and replaced by concrete bases for holiday chalets – the crabstones of the old winches having been removed, and the shafts filled to ground level. It is unfortunate that Rodney Legg's plea for the preservation of this unique area was not heeded by the local authorities.

However, I now write in the hope that something of Swanage's stone industry can still be preserved. For just west of the Council caravan site, above Belle Vue Farm, is what I believe to be the only complete stone quarry remaining in Purbeck. All the quarry houses (with their work benches) are intact, and still surround the towpath. Several retain their stone roofs, and others are covered with rusty corrugated sheeting. The crabstones and their wooden capstan supports remain in position, while the capstan itself (still in good condition) lies in the horse's shed. The entrance to the shaft and its slide – the slope into the underground – also appear excellently preserved, though covered in undergrowth.

The quarry's survival is largely due to the fact that up to two or three years ago the buildings were used by the landowner for sheltering his cattle, but since then the quarry has been fenced off and nature has taken over completely. The corrugated sheeting on one roof has rusted through and caused a sizeable section to collapse. The land on which these workings stand can be of little practical value to the farmer, and I feel strongly that something should be done soon to preserve them before the process of decay takes a firm grip. With a small group of volunteers, perhaps enlisting members of the Langton Preservation Society, it would be possible to clear the undergrowth, repair the buildings, and replace the capstan. This could even be turned into an open-air museum of quarrying history, at a bare minimum of financial investment. It has the added advantage of standing beside the area's main public footpath, the Priest's Way.

During my explorations of the Cowlease hillside, in 1971, I recorded a second shaft lying west of the spur off Manwell Road and a short distance beyond the buildings. This was a more delicate example of stone mine architecture with the hole having a diameter of 12 feet, its edges carefully rounded and the usual slanting shaft, 7 feet 6 inches wide, projecting outward to the north where the hillside gradually fell away. The top 15 feet of the shaft could be seen and the rest was filled with earth and rubbish. Its walls were vertical, built upon the bedrock about 10 feet below ground level and in a style similar to the drystone walls of Purbeck fields. The first stones were laid upright all round the shaft, except the slide part, and each stone was about 20 inches high and 4 inches across. On this line, smaller horizontal walling stones, roughly uniform in size, were placed carefully in level layers. The mine entrance was overhung by thick ivy and adjoined by the foundations of small square sheds.

The picture was very different as recently as 1920 when a few lanes were still in use and blocks were tied to low, sturdy carts of elm and hauled by chains to the head of the shaft. Each lane then had its capstan, with a horse providing the power to pull a wooden bar which gave the leverage to turn the drum of the capstan. The bar was called a spack and required the horse or mule to plod endlessly along a circular towpath.

The Townsend quarries had the deepest lanes in Purbeck, the largest capstans, and the longest spacks. For 200 years it was the biggest production centre of stone in Purbeck and yet its situation came through simple convenience. Standing above the bay, at the back of Peveril and Durlston, Cowlease and Townsend were only yards from old Swanage and its labour force of quarrymen, who were a significant proportion of the adult males in an expanding population, which rose from 1773 in 1831 to 1971 in 1841 and then, in 1851, which was the year of the Great Exhibition, jumped to 3742 inhabitants.

Only when business became a struggle, with the danger of over-working the Swanage quarries, did the trade spread west to Langton. Here the stone came to within 20 feet of the surface without the need to grope through 12 feet of useless cinder in the

bowels of the earth in order to reach a much thinner band of usable caps. Langton quarrymen could concentrate on freestone and downs-vein without the need, except in one location, for venturing deep in search of the harder strata below. One of the most scarred hills near Acton, where the National Trust has restored Norman's Quarry, was called Mount Misery, and looks across to a greener rise which is still known as Mount Pleasant.

Dr C. le Neve Foster, Inspector of Mines for the West of England, carried out a postal survey of the Swanage and Langton quarrymen. He reported in 1878:

The Purbeck stone is a new feature of my statistics. In spite of a great many difficulties, I believe I have at last attained a fairly correct statement of the total amount raised for mines. There are nearly a hundred stone mines in the Swanage district, worked by one, two, or three men underground, who are in many cases the owners as well as the occupiers. Their work is often most irregular; if the men can find work as masons they abandon their quarries for a time, and do not return to them till other work is slack. As the quarrymen of the Isle of Purbeck have never been troubled with Government forms till this year I had considerable difficulty in getting returns from them. Endless mistakes were made, requiring investigation by correspondence, and I may safely say that the 92 stone mines near Swanage, employing only 264 persons, gave me more trouble than all the other mines in my district put together. No doubt I shall have much less inconvenience in future years, as the men will soon get into the way of filling up the returns correctly. The following figures represent the number of tons raised during the past year. Purbeck stone and marble, dressed – 11 816 tons 10 cwt. Purbeck stone, undressed – 1411 tons 10 cwt.

The creation of these quarries came about after 1650 when the medieval basis and traditions of the old Purbeck stone and marble trade were finally shattered. Corfe Castle, its walls in ruins, ceased to be its workshop and distribution centre. The ancient track to Ower Quay was abandoned and the trade no longer looked to Poole Harbour as its natural outlet. Instead the first major mines were sunk above the bay at Swanage and cliff quarries started within the next century at Durlston, Tilly Whim and Winspit. By the 19th century the coastal quarries extended to Dancing Ledge, Hedbury and Seacombe. The scale of the new operations was vast in comparison with the old and some 50 000 tons of stone were shipped from Swanage in the busiest years.

The ideal place for a cliff quarry was where the sea had cut across a valley opening, such as at Tilly Whim Caves where in a gully below Anvil Point, Tilly was probably the original quarry owner of galleries cut into the steep hillside. There was also a

Tilly Mead in Swanage, north of the High Street, between Purbeck House and what is now Station Road. The whim was a derrick mounted on the edge of the cliff and similar to those used today for lowering boats into the sea near Portland Bill. Tilly Whim Quarry – not yet romanticised as Tilly Whim Caves – is mentioned in a letter of 13 April 1813:

There is so much room in this quarry for any assignable number of men to work, and so great a facility, in summer, of shipping the goods, letting them down at once by a crane into the vessel, that the men of industry and enterprise ought to command almost the whole market for the species of articles which this quarry produces... The sort of goods which the quarry yields are of what is called the Purbeck-Portland, a sort of freestone; much like the Portland, only harder, and much used for buildings, in bridges, harbours, fortification walls, troughs, columns, rollers, staddlestones, etc.

Calculations of the output of Tilly Whim have been made from a series of accounts dated between 1805 and 1812. The total production of the quarry for the five-year period ending on Lady Day in 1810 appears to have been:

37 setts of brigs and caps
14 setts of rick-stones
83 pairs of staddle-stones
340.5 pecks of sinks and troughs
318.5 feet of rollers
2305 tons of backing
97 tons of blocks
133 tons of pitchers

The majority of farm granaries in southern England were built on Dorset rick-stones or staddle-stones. Most of them had either nine or a dozen staddles with a timber structure on top. Charles Vancouver reported to the Board of Agriculture, from Hampshire, in 1813:

A very excellent practice seems to be fast gaining ground in many parts of the county, of building wheat barns, as well as corn stacks in general, upon stone stands or staddles, the stones, or legs and caps (as they are usually called) are supplied from the quarries of Purbeck and Portland, and cost at the seaports or wharves at the head of the marine navigation, about seven shillings per pair.

Even in the far-off summers of the old stone trade it was no straightforward task getting worked loads of cut stone from the Townsend quarries to ships standing offshore in the bay. The blocks could be handled five times before they were sailing towards

Showpiece cliff-quarry, graced with Shakespearean verse by George Burt and opened as a Victorian tourist attraction, named Tilly Whim Caves.

the customer. Old Swanage was a quarrying town and the stone came down cart tracks to the quarry entrance at Cowlease. From here it was hauled along the High Street, between close-packed lines of cottages at The Narrows, to stacks of stone – known as bankers – in compounds by the shore. The High Street was hazardous for pedestrians and carriages.

War and accidents enter the story. Drownings were common, particularly among those bringing loaded stone boats around from the west, and coming to grief in turbulent water off the rocky ledges of Peveril Point. Here the cross-currents claimed the life of John Norman in August 1836, the day before he was to have married, when the sea swamped his father's craft.

During the Napoleonic Wars, two Swanage stonemasons, Isaac May and William Melmoth, are said to have been captured by French privateers while they were loading stone in a boat and were held hostage for several months. One of the carters from the quarries was injured in an accident in October 1881. The *Dorset County Chronicle* reported:

Last week as Mr Grant's carter, called Pitcher, was coming down the hill from the quarries with three horses and a wagon and about four tons of stone, the tackle for tying up the hind wheel broke and, the weight forcing on the wagon, the carter was knocked down, and the wheels going over both legs broke them. Fortunately the shafts of the wagon striking against the side wall checked and stopped it, or some of the horses might have been killed. The poor carter, in great suffering, is [sic], we hear, progressing but slowly, though, we hope, favourably, under the care and treatment of Dr G.C. Delamotte. We regret to hear Pitcher is not in any friendly society.

Two weeks later, 'the poor carter Pitcher' died, when 'lockjaw set in'.

The town's 19th-century visitors avoided the streets where stone wagons raised clouds of white, choking dust throughout the best days of summer. Ruts and runnels were inches deep. In winter the streets became quagmires of yellow clay. Horses hauled the carts to the quayside bankers where each load joined the vast piles of stone and much would be re-worked. Some 60 loads a day, each matching carter Pitcher's three or four tons, came to the water's edge. Some stacks of stone stood ten feet high and they stretched along the south-eastern edge of the town from the Royal Victoria Hotel around to the Mowlem Institute.

Charles Edmund Robinson, writing in 1882, described the bankers and visualised their demise, but his prediction of the replacement by seafront pleasure gardens was wishful thinking, for bricks and mortar would take the place of the stone. He hoped that the coming of the railway 'would set the bankers free'. Robinson's town had:

... unsightly wharves, piled high with stone, which extend some 100 yards along the curve of the bay, directly in front of the principal terrace, and excluding all view of the sea from anyone walking on the pavement. Here, on raised platforms intersected by wagon-roads, are stored the wrought stones of every kind, which have been carted down to the merchants from the quarries on the hill where they were dug, and here they remain until the day of shipment; when a cargo hurriedly leaves the bankers, only to be replaced by newly-collected loads. Even more destructive of the amenities of Swanage as a watering place than its narrow inconvenient old streets, are these bankers occupying and disfiguring as they do the very spot where pretty gardens, with broad gravelly paths, should be laid out as a public seaside promenade.

High-wheeled stone carts waited at the bankers, to be loaded with stone, and were drawn by horses down to the beach and into the sea. The stone was then transferred into barges to be rowed out to ships standing in the bay. These barges were purpose-built and pointed at stem and stern, so they did not have to be turned around, and though cumbersome they carried immense stones, including some weighing half a ton. Manned by two men with oars, the boats also had a small lug-sail, for when the wind was favourable. They ferried a load of six to nine tons on each journey. The stone was shipped differently from Durlston Bay. Here the stone boats were hauled close inshore and an inclined stage placed nearby. The blocks of stone were then slid down the ramp and lowered into the waiting boat, helped along by quarrymen who often stood waist deep in the sea for hours.

As well as taking stone out, the barges were also a lifeline into the town, bringing ashore coal and other supplies from coasters anchored in the bay. In the middle of the 19th century there were on average 70 stone-craft operating at Swanage and in an easterly gale and during the hardest weather all boats were hauled ashore and safely grounded. It was a wet and tricky job, only possible by using capstans, rollers and chains, but a vital one because the barges could soon be overwhelmed and sink.

The sight of tall carts being pulled by horses into the sea, out to the waiting barges, was not the only remarkable scene in Swanage during the first half of the 19th century. Stones from the Townsend quarries were used for barter with a 12lb block being worth a penny and a dozen of them equal to a shilling. William Masters Hardy described their use:

I have seen quarrymen carrying stones on their backs from the quarries to pay for their beer, baccy, and other commodities. Land, coals, bread, boots, clothes, and almost every article required for home consumption could be bought with stone currency.

Horse-drawn carts, stone lighters and ketches in Swanage Bay, painted by M. Croft in 1869, also showing the stone quay and timber pier, and Coastguard lookout on Peveril Point.

A perfectly composed Walter Pouncy photograph with two gentlemen walking southwards along the beach in 1888 as stone is transferred from a cart (far right) into a barge to be taken to the Brisk (offshore), with the Nile being beached.

Stone Bankers

Left: *Looking east from the stone bankers, to the stone quay, which is hosting the 1888 regatta, with the Clock Tower behind.*

Right: *Stone bankers, seen from the stone quay, in a view looking north-west with buildings around the White Swan and Albion Place visible in the distance.*

Left: *Street kerbing (left) and other cut stone awaiting shipment from the bankers, in a photograph of circa 1890, looking north-east to Ballard Point with the seaward gable end of the Mowlem Institute (far left).*

Right: *View over the stone bankers from John Mowlem's Observatory, above Victoria Terrace, to his 1863-built Mowlem Institute (central building) and empty countryside northwards to the Ulwell Gap, c.1870.*

Stone Bankers

Above: *Stone bankers, with workshop and derrick, showing the slipway (centre) down which stone was exported, in a photograph looking north-east in about 1890.*

Right: *Shoreline profile of the stone bankers, stacked high to the very edge of the sea wall, in a shot of the central shore, looking south, in about 1885.*

Northern extremity of the stone bankers, extending beyond the Mowlem Institute (right) in a pre-1895 view looking southwards to the stone quay (centre) and 1859-built pier and Clock Tower (far left).

Bowler hats were then being worn by the quarrymen, along with moleskin trousers, which were said to be 'fine things for underground'. Above ground, however, they recalled the surprising heaviness after they had been caught by a sudden downpour. Made not from the skin of moles, but from a strong cotton fustian – the pile of which is shaved – the trousers lasted for years. They can withstand rough treatment and are still worn by foundry workers, another endangered species, to protect their legs from sparks. Moleskins were baggy leggings of brownish-white thick cloth known as fustian (called 'fuskin' in Purbeck). It could be washed, but never dry-cleaned, though it was always considered better just to leave it alone. Then, having been worn to shape, the trousers were usually hung 'at ease' ready to be stepped into.

I interviewed Nelson Thomson, one of the older quarrymen living and working at Acton, in 1970. He used to have moleskins and could also remember when quarrymen were still wearing their traditional bowler hats:

When they built the sea wall down at Swanage in 1904, there's quite a lot of those men then [he pointed to a photograph] wearing a real hard bowler hat. You could take one and play football with it. I could remember my father wearing one on special days and I could go back to the early 1920s and there was quite a lot of the old men still wearing them. We did have a bowler hat dug up from one of the quarries up here when one of the men got out [after an accident underground] and never got hurted. But he did leave a bowler hat down there and later we went and touched it; it all fell to pieces. That was up here on top, opposite Gallows Gore, back in the 1920s.

I used to work with a man named Billy Brown back in 1922 and he used to wear a bowler hat. He used to go to church and Wareham Market and wear his bowler hat. Billy Brown was living down in Langton village and he used to work up at the cliff quarries. He was nearly 80 when he died and he bin dead nearly 40 years. I went into the stone trade in 1925. I had to pay £5.7s.6d. and a penny loaf and a quart of beer. Real tasty job in those days. In the little village hall at Corfe, and I had to go down and kick the ball up through the Aves [The Halves], as they do call it. I was the last one to be married into the trade and I had to kick the football – the last place to kick the ball, the villagers could go and pick en up and take en away. That was the quarryman's right for that day...

Such ancient rights and customs were the subject of a report by the Government's Inspectors of Factories and Workshops, issued in March 1880. This was reported in *The Globe* newspaper and referred to the 'islanders' of Purbeck and Portland as remarkable in their habits and having:

... a settled idea that the workings of the quarries in those localities is a privilege of their own, and they not only resent the intrusion of other workmen but go so far as to qualify the latter and, indeed, the whole world outside Purbeck and Portland, by the opprobrious title of foreigners. The Purbeckians of Swanage maintain that this privilege is secured to them by an ancient charter providing that no person may establish himself in their trade who is not a direct descendant of some local quarryman.

The Inspector goes on to describe various non-bureaucratic immunities claimed by the islanders:

Both peoples have a strong objection to being interfered with, the Purbeckians especially holding a sort of tradition that they are beyond all laws, and that they would have a sort of right to make regulations for their own government, the general sum of which appears to be to arrange that they should do as much, or as little, work as they please, have unlimited beer, and send their offspring to school, or not, at discretion, which would result in about 90 per cent growing up uneducated as their parents boast that they are themselves.

So tenacious are both races of their individuality that they will not even contract matrimonial alliances with the foreigner, but intermarry amongst themselves so that nearly everybody in both locations is related to everybody else. Notwithstanding this fact, it appears that the evils which are generally supposed to result from intermarriage are not particularly noticeable but, on the contrary, the health of the community is so good that no one could fail to be struck by their unusually fine appearance, and at Portland boys of 13 or 14 are often found to look as if they were two years older.

In a court case in 1880 it was heard that a young boy, Jesse Stickland, was working full time dressing stone at Swanage and had not been sent to school. It was said in his father's defence that Swanage quarrymen were under the impression that:

... lads working in the mines do not come under the Elementary Education Act. They thought the Inspector was carrying out the spirit of an obnoxious act which was hostile to them. They think they can do what they like with their own children.

Though the case was found to be proved, no fine was imposed, as the magistrates merely 'wished the defendants to comply with the law of the country' and simply ordered payment of costs. It was pointed out by the Inspector that stone workers were permitted to send their children to work at ten years old, provided they kept them at school half time, until full-time employment at the age of 13.

The Masonic Hall (lettering over-written for 'Water Office') in Marshall Row was the social power-base for George Burt and friends, in the United Fraternity of Free and Accepted Masons of England.

George Burt, one of the Justices, remarked that Purbeck men were rather strong-headed but he would advise them to look upon the Inspector as a friend rather than an enemy. The Inspector replied: 'We are on the best terms except when it comes to keeping the law!' The Earl of Eldon supported the backlash against the Education Act and was in the chair at a meeting of the Wareham and Purbeck Union which came out in favour of ending 'the compulsory sending to school by the labouring and industrial classes of children after the age of 12, and allowing their full employment at that age.'

Langton Matravers burial registers show that several children met horrible deaths in the more confined mines. One old quarryman told a Swanage historian, John T. Dean: 'They wuss cheap, plenty of 'em, and more wur they come vrom.'

Purbeck also provides an example of industrial trade restrictions in action in the 1860s. Four lads were thrown out of work in the quarries because the operatives' trades union, the Company of Marblers and Stonecutters, disapproved of their employment – fearing the boys would deprive their members of jobs. Nathan Chinchen White is the signatory, and the document is witnessed by two wardens of the company, Richard Benfield and another of more difficult signature. It was signed in Swanage, on 29 March 1865, and was sent to me by Peter Hill. It reads:

I do hereby agree with the wardens of the Company of Marblers and Stonecutters of the Isle of Purbeck, to discharge from my employ on Saturday 1st April 1865 two lads viz Dowland and Cole. I further agree to discharge from my employ in June 1865 one lad viz Damon. I also further agree to discharge from my employ of June 1866 one lad viz Milehall. Frederick Arney to continue in my employ but not to become a member of the Company. I also further agree not to employ any more lads contrary to the wish of the said Company of Marblers and Stonecutters.

These openings in the ground were sometimes more than mere work holes. Several of those around Langton and Acton were used until 1930 as sources of fresh water for the cottages. Men and women queued for their turn to descend 20 feet with a bucket. John Dean was told by a quarryman that the stone and underpicking dirts effectively provided quick filter-beds: 'Fellow cud 'ave a crap anner piss one wick. Tu, three wicks later ee'd draw it up from thic well, all viltered and reel sweet.'

The old shafts are still there, though mainly stopped up at the entrance, and one was re-opened at Webber's Quarry to reveal air so foul that no candle would burn there. Experiences such as these belong to an era that has vanished, having been replaced by open-pit excavations, as mechanisation, safety, and animal welfare legislation ended a way of life. The last of a dying generation tell of how the depth of the

shafts could be gauged by the size of their capstans. These were tough pieces of machinery, requiring only an occasional greasing of the gudgeon, which could last a human lifetime and wear out several old mules in the process.

Langton's capstans were quite small, to tackle shallow workings, and could be worked by a donkey harnessed to the spack. Or an old pony could wind a ton up the quarry shaft as it walked at the end of a 16-foot beam around a 6-foot elm capstan. Such an arrangement was said to raise one ton by six feet for each circuit that the animal made. When a loaded cart reached the top of the slide, the pony would be unharnessed from the spack, and attached directly to the cart. It was then hauled to the working floor.

The usual place for the donkey or pony – or horse or mule at Swanage where workings were deeper – was a shed beside the towpath, adjoining the opening of the mine shaft. Non availability of horsepower at Swanage as recently as 1850 resulted in two girls having to tread the spack, 'as their father was an old man and had no one to help him, his daughters were compelled to walk round and round in the mud and clay up to their ankles.'

The collateral benefit of honeycombing Swanage and southern Purbeck with a network of underground tunnels and lanes, in a location blessed with a mild maritime climate, has been to establish the area as a nationally important stronghold for bats. The quarry shafts and coastal galleries have provided extensive hiding and hibernation places. Purbeck hosts the widest range of British species and some of the densest populations.

Most of the abandoned mines have been at least partially blocked by dumped cars and other rubbish. Hibernating bats are also vulnerable to disturbance or vandalism. One malicious person or heartless action can kill an entire population of hundreds in less than an hour.

For instance the mouse-eared bat, making its only entry in British records, was discovered in a Purbeck quarry in 1956. The entrance was then bulldozed and the colony lost though another may have been established as the species has been seen in Dorset since. Some 17 different species have been found in Winspit alone where iron grills now protect the main entrance. Bernard Gooch carried out pioneering work in abandoned underground lanes at Swanage, now mainly closed and lying beneath hillside caravans, in the 1940s. Eastwards, between Manwell Road and Mount Scar, the undulating scrublands have been protected by Dorset Wildlife Trust.

Gooch found that badgers, foxes and rabbits also used the deep shafts, and measured a constant underground temperature of 50 degrees fahrenheit in cases where one tunnel received draughts from another. These were suitable for living and breeding purposes but the situation was different for hibernating bats.

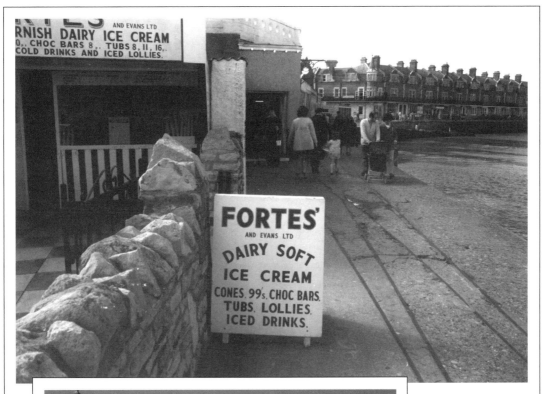

*Fortes' ice cream
and the points of
the Victorian stone
tramway, photographed
by Colin Graham from
the east, showing the
Edwardian balconies
of The Parade that
arose in 1905 from the
rubble of the bankers
beside Institute Road.*

They needed a lower temperature. To achieve this it was necessary for blockages to have taken place between one quarry system and the next. Such cul-de-sac hollows, where the air no longer circulated, provided lower temperatures which the bats would seek out in autumn for hibernation places.

The Siberian winter of 1947 was particularly good for milestone records in the Purbeck quarries. Bechstein's bat made its first appearance. Likewise the common serotine bat, already familiar in the evening sky, was recorded for the first time underground, in a cave or a mine, in the British Isles. Five were hibernating from the severe cold. Gooch found that the much rarer greater horseshoe bat was the commonest species under the ground.

He also made a surprising discovery which indicates how bats choose their stopping off points amid complete darkness. It also explains why nature often fails to provide suitable habitats in the way that man does so well. Cave-like lanes provided ample foot-holds, and had bats flying along them, but none were hanging from what seemed to be ideal positions for them to use.

Time and again he returned to bat-free quarry lanes and observed that:

These neglected or deserted lanes had one feature in common – rough, untidy quarry walls. The latter are generally neatly made of relatively large blocks of stone, or they may consist of solid rock, both of which the bats use, as well as the ceiling, when looking for somewhere to hang. Has this avoidance of lanes of rough, or rubbly, walls anything

to do perhaps with the bats' echo-location requirements? Emitting a series of ultra-sonic squeaks as they fly along these pitch-dark lanes, they receive perhaps confusing or disconcerting echoes. [As a result they choose] ...to hang up in lanes where echo-location proves easiest.

Swanage naturalist Leonard Tatchell, driven by heavy rain to seek refuge in a cave at Winspit, found himself investigating a quarry that had not been worked for many years:

After getting accustomed to the semi-darkness I began to explore and, looking up, I saw about a score of the common horseshoe bat, and going further I found that the roof of this working was teeming with hundreds of the creatures, and the odour was not pleasant. I amused myself by throwing up small stones and got many of them flying.

The last sentence is no longer acceptable behaviour!

Perhaps the most touching of Dorset epitaphs is a large boulder of Purbeck stone in old workings beside the Priest's Way near Belle Vue Farm. It was erected by quarryman Werney Bonfield, who built Providence Terrace, Swanage, towards the end of Victoria's reign:

Beneath this stone lies our mule. She was a faithful creature, drawing up the stone from this quarry for 32 years. Died aged 34 years. Also our little cat named Too Too who followed her master from this quarry to his home and back for 20 years. RIP.

Quarr houses, crabstones, capstan and slide in Alfred Dawson's drawing of a typical Swanage stone mine, in 1882.

Chapter 6

FISHING AND FERRYING

Detail of a fisherman's cottage in Station Road, from the south-west, with nets and floats being stretched out from the fence beside the side door and running between the male figures.

Quarrying for many was regarded as winter work. Summer was for fishing, plus a short autumn season for what became dried herrings, smoked and cured in sheds established by William Morton Pitt in 1788. Shorter nights were also for smuggling. Not for nothing were the fishermen's cottages that used to stand on the north side of the seaward end of Station Road depicted as 'Smugglers' Cottages' in Edwardian postcards. Everyone was doing it along the Dorset coast, or so it must have seemed throughout the 18th and early-19th centuries as excise duties and the blockades of incessant European squabbles created crimes that few saw as offending against natural justice. Purbeck was a remote corner of the coast along which kegs of spirits and cases of tea could be landed and concealed.

The problem then was their onward transportation, usually across Poole Harbour but sometimes brazenly through the middle of Wareham, into mainland Dorset and northwards along tracks and droveways as they gained added value on reaching Moonraker country in Wiltshire. As always in legally dubious activities, it is the failures we hear about, and smuggling historian Roger Guttridge's roll-of-honour for Swanage has just four names of those who went through the courts. They are from good old Purbeck families.

Swanage seaman Thomas Dyke had already been imprisoned for an alleged 'breach of the peace' in 1815 and would then be fined £100 for smuggling in 1819. He was taken to Portsmouth and put on board HMS *Queen Charlotte* 'to be impressed into His Majesty's Royal Navy'. That was at the age of 58. George Rolles, a 45-year-old labourer, was fined £100 and sentenced to a year in Dorchester Gaol in 1824. Then, towards the end of the smuggling era in 1841, two Swanage shoemakers were caught together and each sentenced to six months' imprisonment. They were 45-year-old John Briggs and 39-year-old Trelevan Haysom.

William Masters Hardy collected dozens of mainly light-hearted anecdotes and romanticised the illicit trade for Edwardian readers. Preventive officers, and sometimes the smugglers themselves, knew that there was a thin line between excitement and violence. Customs officers Milner and Shank, stationed at Swanage in 1760, had a close shave when they heard gunfire offshore. Eight smugglers then came ashore and said they were fleeing from a midnight engagement between two smuggling cutters and Royal Navy warships. They had lost their goods but escaped being impressed. The Customs officers hired a boat and three oarsmen and sailed out to one of the smuggling vessels, telling its Captain, John Harman, that they were taking it and its cargo of contraband to Poole Quay. The naval officers had other ideas. They were under orders to take their prize to Sandown, on the Isle of Wight, or into Portsmouth. The Swanage boat was threatened with being blown out of the water if it continued with the seizure. Argument resulted in the compromise that Shank, as well, would accompany the captured cutter to Portsmouth, where the Swanage officer would be overruled and told that the Navy had possession, both physically and legally.

The fishing hamlet of Swanage formerly clustered along the southern side of an inlet and backwater that stretched inland, westwards, for a mile. This was along The Brook (it lacked a specific name because there was no need for one) which flows from Harman's Cross and widened into marshland in a strip along the northern side, beside Tilly Mead and across the area that would be transformed by the

Exemption certificate of 19-year-old Swanage fisherman Francis Haysom, freeing him from being pressed into naval service during the Napoleonic Wars, issued at Poole on 10 April 1810.

building of the railway line in 1884. Houses along the north side of the High Street had long gardens descending to a series of gateways in their bottom boundaries, which formed what David Lewer calls 'the Great Wall of Swanage', with fishermen's moorings beyond. Iron eye-rings have been discovered set in surviving sections of wall that are now a considerable distance from the nearest standing water.

Some were at the Barley Mow and beside the Town Hall where The Drong alleyway led to the backwater. It could only be worked at high tide, when stone barges were hauled upstream, to a loading point between central Herston and what is now King George's Field, in the region of Prospect Farm. Reputedly, a century or so earlier, there was a shipping wharf much further up the valley, between Quince Hill Wood and the buildings of New Barn. This is two miles west of the town, on the 40-feet contour, and would have been well above any help from the tides.

The seaward end of the backwater is not that much easier to trace. Its mouth extended across the site of what is now The Mowlem and had a quay on the south side, where The Parade was built in 1905. Here stood a pair of stone-roofed cottages that were inundated, being partially washed away, at 02.00 hours on 29 December 1848. Tragedy, caused by a combination of adverse natural circumstances, ended the Soper family's Christmas.

John Mowlem, that pivotal figure in Swanage history whose family shaped its modern face, records in his diary that a fierce sea had been holding back tidal water in the backwater at the same time as a torrent streamed down the valley. Easterly winds and waves prevented this ever-growing volume of water from draining into the bay. Then:

... after three hours ebb-tide, such was the rush of water by The Brook that it undermined the foundation of a house in the occupation of Mr John Soper, master of the cutter Gertrude, *that the front fell into The Brook and Mrs Soper fell with it.*

She was found, drowned, on the shore opposite Mowlem's home. Against 'great difficulty' James Pushman led a valiant rescue operation and succeeded in saving the lives of the Sopers' two daughters and their two female lodgers.

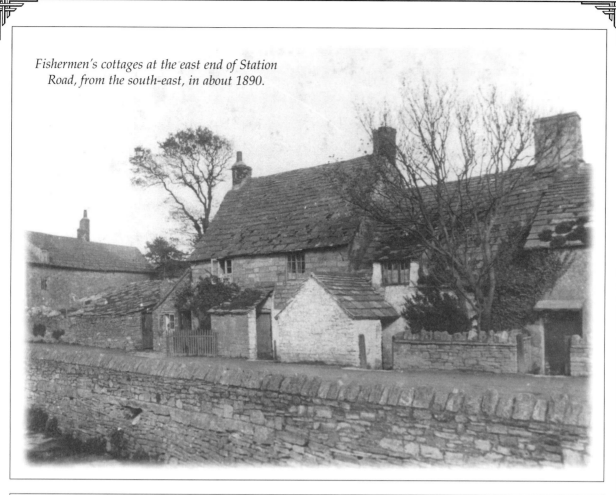

*Fishermen's cottages at the east end of Station
Road, from the south-east, in about 1890.*

*The Boat Haul in the estuary of The Brook at Swanage, painted by William Daniell in 1823,
for his four-volume work published in 1825 as* A Voyage round Great Britain.

Left: *Eldon Terrace inundated in the flash-flood of 9 March 1914.*

Below: *Flooding in November 1935 along Lower High Street and Institute Road.*

Below: *Boating through King's Road East during the 1935 flood, with a sign for Joseph Parsons & Son, builders (right of lamppost).*

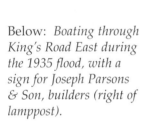

Historically, the only crossing point – giving name to Northbrook Road on the other side – was below St Mary's Church. Here, beside Swanwic House, is the only urban section of The Brook that has not been put into a culvert. It proceeds beneath the shops under the north side of Station Road, and took its revenge on the town by flowing through the streets on several occasions through the 20th century, notably in March 1914, November 1935, and on 3 February 1990.

The first, which peaked on 9 March 1914, was caused by a weekend of heavy rain. Rising water from The Brook overflowed across the churchyard, flooded the rectory, and then swept down King's Road East and along Eldon Terrace, to reach the sea via the wharf at the end of the High Street. Thomas Powell photographed boats in Eldon Terrace for the *Western Gazette*, which reported:

The photograph indicates the scenes in Eldon Terrace, where in the course of an hour the water in the houses rose to a height of four feet. Many of the occupants were forced to retreat to the upper rooms, hardly having time to save any furniture before the flood came. Messrs J. Smith and Son's drapery stores facing King's Road suffered severely, the plate-glass window being broken and a quantity of goods damaged. Boats were hastily brought from the quay, and went into the shop through the broken window, and the occupants of the boats saved a lot of the goods by handing them upstairs to the assistants. The grocery stores owned by Mr A.E. Turner also suffered severely. The Station Road was also flooded, the water coming through the stone-yards of Messrs Parsons and Hayter into the side road by the premises of Mr C.H. Mitchell, flooding the road almost from the corner of Institute Road to Mr Crump's, the tobacconist's, and the Post Office was compelled to close between three and six o'clock. Towards five o'clock the water began to subside almost as rapidly as it rose, and by ten o'clock it had gone. All Monday night and the greater part of Tuesday the Fire Brigade were engaged in pumping the water out from the cellars of the business premises in Institute Road.

The Brook normally flows into the bay on the south side of the Mowlem Theatre. Flood control measures, in 1992–93, saw an additional storm-water culvert being constructed beneath Victoria Avenue, with its outfall being beneath a large raised extension to the beach at the bottom end of The Avenue.

As for the most famous of local products, from Lulworth around to Poole, Swanage received its earliest advertisement from the amazing Celia Fiennes, one of the earliest female explorers. She travelled through Purbeck on her 'Great Journey' around Britain in 1698–99. She had a passion for chemistry and manufacturing processes that could only be eclipsed by 'lobsters and crabs and shrimps'. Those from Brownsea Island and Worbarrow Bay were very good. But from Swanage they were the best she would ever eat in her life.

Offshore, monkfish are common in Swanage waters, with an extraordinary specimen of four-feet-six-inches length having been caught by a yachtsman near Peveril Point in June 1892. It was two-feet, six inches in breadth. On being cut open it was found to be a pregnant female containing '22 young ones, each measuring 10 inches in length and five inches across'.

For the ferry to Poole, people from Purbeck walked to the harbour shore, with one of the oldest services in Dorset being that from Redhorn Quay on the western side of the South Haven Peninsula. It has the remains of bankers of stone to show that like Ower, the ferry point from Corfe Castle, it also served Purbeck's principal trade. It was described for me by Ben Pond in 1972:

It is composed of huge, square-cut stone, tier upon tier, with deep water alongside. Fifty odd years ago there were deep wheel ruts leading across to the quay. Slowly, Redhorn Channel has silted at its entrance, from South Deep, since 1922.

Other stones, found in the mud of the harbour shore and towards Goathorn, include granite boulders brought as ballast. In the mid 1970s, having opened up deep-Channel fishing with Graham Ingham, Peter Haine became the first man to catch a ton of lobster in a day.

Crab and lobster pots on the stone quay, with the fisherman chatting to quarryman (John Coffin) – the latter in standard work dress of mole-skins and bowler-hat, in a Walter Pouncy study, c.1895.

Mowlem's Column

Mowlem's Column, cannon-bollards, and Beach Road, looking northwards towards the Grand Hotel in a view c.1895 with the main notice prohibiting 'Removal of sand, shingle, stone, or other materials from the fore-shore'.

IN COMMEMORATION
OF A
GREAT NAVAL BATTLE
FOUGHT WITH THE DANES
IN SWANAGE BAY
BY ALFRED THE GREAT
A.D. 877

Re-set on a plinth, Mowlem's Column now dominates the promenade, looking north-west towards Ballard Point, with an inscription on the other side to commemorate a 'great naval battle' that never happened.

Chapter 7

MASONRY AND MONUMENTS

Monumental Swanage began with a squat obelisk which formerly stood in the High Street, on the north side of the road, above Court Hill. It was erected by contractor John Mowlem, who was born in a cottage down the hill, in memory of Prince Albert (1819–61). Queen Victoria's consort had visited Swanage in 1849. J.G. Harrod's *Directory of Dorsetshire* (1865) heaps fulsome praise upon what was known as 'The Albert Memorial':

Small as Swanage is at present, it has displayed, in proportion to its limits, a highly loyal patriotic feeling. In doing justice to the memory of Albert the Good, the inhabitants were amongst the foremost. A very chaste and well-proportioned obelisk, with an appropriate inscription, was erected by the north side of the road above the Cemetery, at a point where it is seen for a considerable distance in either direction of the highway, and at once forms a beautiful foreground object to the view of the valley, and a very interesting one in all the views from it.

Maybe, but it was never held in high esteem by the town, and the pyramid would be removed in the 1930s. The steps and plinth, with its simple inscription to 'ALBERT THE GOOD' and his dates, were demolished in 1971 after a dispute with developers. In 1991 I rediscovered its remains, stacked in sections, in St Aldhelm's Quarry, near St Alban's Head. No one showed much interest in returning it to Swanage. The town had tired of its late-Victorian epithet 'London by Sea' which arose from the immense quantities of masonry and monuments that were shipped back to the town by its three national building contractors. John Mowlem's example was followed with increasing zeal by George Burt and Thomas Docwra.

The seafront granite column on the north side of the Mowlem Institute was constructed by John Mowlem in 1862 to give Swanage a place in history. It commemorates an alleged battle between the Saxons and Danes in Swanage Bay. Sir Frederick Treves, writing his *Highways and Byways in Dorset*, in 1906, drew attention to the incongruity of the four cannon balls which are balanced on top:

Amongst other litter in the London contractor's yard

there would seem to have been some cannon balls. The faithful pavior [stone-paver] evidently had some difficulty in working these in for the adornment of his birthplace. Cannon balls suggest battle, but there has been no battle at Swanage. King Alfred, however, is supposed to have defeated the Danes in Swanage Bay in the year of our Lord 877. Naturally enough, the contractor erected a pillar on the Marine Parade to commemorate this proud if dim event, and placed the cannon balls on top of it. To some these missiles may appear inappropriate, as gunpowder was not invented until more than 400 years after the assumed engagement.

These words were turned against the monument at the meeting of Swanage Urban District Council in October 1965 when Councillor A.E.R. Gray said it was an object of general ridicule. Not only was the claim of a battle historically inaccurate, but the cannon balls looked like a pawnbroker's sign: 'The day of monuments has passed. This one should be demolished and sunk to the bottom of the bay.'

Fortunately for the survival of the folly, his fellow Council members voted to spend £200 on moving the column out of the way of a development on the promenade, rather than a bargain price of £75 for its demolition and removal. It should have been pointed out that the cannon balls had seen real battle. They are unexploded 13-inch Russian shells brought back to Portsmouth in 1857 – in the sides of wooden battleships – from engagements fought by the Royal Navy in the Black Sea and the Baltic, during the Crimean War. They are set in a triangular arrangement with three cannon balls having a fourth balanced on top. There is said to have been a fifth, that fell off years ago and was eventually washed up near Old Harry Rocks.

Swanage also has its make-believe cannon. From the 1750s, real cannon were utilised on street corners and at busy pinch-points in the City of London, being set vertically into the ground to keep wagons on the carriageway and prevent them damaging the footway. The supply kept up with demand during the Napoleonic Wars, from 1793 to 1815, when plenty of cracked, captured and obsolete gun-barrels found a second life as street furniture.

Then foundries in London and Staffordshire began making cast-iron imitation cannon. They were smaller than the real thing, without trunnions, and instead had raised rings so that horses could be tethered just below the rounded tops. At the other end, for setting into the ground, the conventional circular cross-sections became square, as this tended to be more stable. As with real cannon, insignia and lettering could be added to the replica by the pattern-maker, which then went into the foundry sand-boxes to make the moulds for molten iron.

Designs developed quickly, away from the simple but elegant copy of a cannon, and each London parish wanted its cannon-bollards to look different from those of the surrounding districts. The original round pattern evolved into square, hexagonal, and even octagonal shapes. These were often further refined with bevels and flutings.

From 1823, when Purbeck contractor John Mowlem began laying raised, kerbed pavements beside the streets in London, many of these bollards became redundant. His successor, George Burt, was shipping them in quantity to Swanage by the 1880s. He must have brought a couple of hundred, at least, as 111 survivors were counted and mapped in 1973. Sidney Tringham, who grew up in Battersea, told me that London schoolboys found their three-feet height perfect for leapfrog and coined the phrase 'pavement guardians' to describe their purpose; he found one in Swanage that did this a little too effectively when wild bees found the hinge-hole made for a perfect

apiary. Many were used to restrict equestrian use of footpaths. Others demarcated the curtilage of monuments or were used as gate-posts. The Great Globe, emplaced in 1887, is surrounded by a ring of such London cannon-bollards. Clockwise from the west side of the top of the seaward steps these are cast with origins as follows:

St Martins 1820
St Martins 1816
St Giles and Bloomsbury
St Giles and Bloomsbury (again)
St Martins 1844
St Martins 1815
St Martins 1816
St Martins 1820
St Giles and Bloomsbury
St Martins 1844
St Martins 1815

Elsewhere, you can find:

St Annes and St Giles
St Annes Soho
Saint George Hanover Square
St Martin-in-the-Fields
St James Clerkenwell
St James Westminster
Christ Church Middlesex
City of London
City of Westminster

The Clock Tower memorial to the Duke of Wellington, with its original spire as removed from beside London Bridge in 1866, seen from the east with the lifeboat slipway in the foreground and 1859-built pier behind.

The Clock Tower, its spire replaced by a cupola in 1904, seen with lobster pots in the foreground in the 1970s.

Emblems include the coats-of-arms of these cities, of London (cross and sword) and Westminster (portcullis), and a crown and 'IV WR', which stands for '4 William Rex'; namely King William IV, who reigned from 1830 to 1837.

As well as cannon posts, Burt literally carted off lamp standards, columns from Billingsgate Market, two statues from the Royal Exchange, and an archway from Grosvenor Square. Any movable landmarks from the London scene were uprooted, dismantled, brought home and put together again at Purbeck House, or placed elsewhere across the town. Size was no problem; one can imagine a latter-day Burt commandeering the Millennium Dome from beside his Greenwich works.

The Wellington Clock Tower is surplus London writ large. It is a magnificent edifice of Victorian gothic, now clock-less, standing at Rockleigh between the Old Pier and Lifeboat Station on the northern side of the Peveril Point promontory. It is the most distinctive structure of seaside Swanage, not that it was designed to be seen here. This was a monument built for the heart of the British Empire, to commemorate the former Prime Minister and victor of the Battle of Waterloo, the first Duke of Wellington, who died in 1852. It was erected beside the Southwark end of London Bridge in 1854, to revive patriotic spirits in the year when Allied fleets headed for war with Russia in the Crimea, to be rewarded by success at the Battle of Alma, but alarmed by the greater reality of Sebastapol seeming impregnable.

The year would be remembered for the Charge of the Light Brigade, at Balaclava, as the most magnificent debacle in military history.

The war, and a revisionist mood towards Wellington and his resistance to electoral reform, brought the Wellington Clock Tower into ridicule. It boasted what had been acclaimed as 'the best clock in the world' when it was made for the Great Exhibition in 1851. This had transparent dials but failed to give accurate time. There was nothing wrong with the mechanism. What made it a laughing stock was constant vibration from the passing carts. The Metropolitan Police also denounced the monument as 'an unwarrantable obstruction' to the traffic at the most congested point in the capital.

It might have survived a little longer but the railway system was fast closing in around it. The building of the viaduct along the south side of Duke Street Hill blocked its principal view in 1863. This brought the trains into the Duke's more lasting memorial at Waterloo East and went on to Hungerford Bridge and Charing Cross.

Demolition took place in 1866. Mowlem and Co. donated it to fellow contractor Thomas Docwra – whose name is still carried on red vans across the country – after he had bought The Grove, also in 1866. He would make his home at Rockleigh in the south-east corner of the bay and re-erected the Clock Tower beside the foreshore at the eastern end of his grounds. Victorian and early Edwardian photographs show that it had an attractive spire.

Other ex-London monuments from Thomas Docwra's rebuilding of The Grove, standing on Peveril Downs.

A religious fanatic objected and this was replaced by a cupola in 1904. The clock never reached Swanage and the circular openings for the dials remain empty. Strangely, at night, they now enable a deeper appreciation of time, when the stonework frames sections of deep space.

Docwra also embellished The Grove, in 1892, with two colossal classical columns, of Greek Revival period fluted supports with delicately carved Ionic capitals. They were set in the forecourt and would be re-erected in splendid isolation on the grassy slope of Peveril Downs after demolition of the Hotel Grosvenor in 1986.

In the town, on the site of the Drong Cottages just down the High Street from Purbeck House, George Burt spent £4500 during 1881–83 in bringing the lofty and richly-carved frontage of the Mercers' Hall from Cheapside, in the City of London, to grace Swanage's new Town Hall. It is a remarkable baroque edifice, dating from 1670, which pulls rank on all home-grown creations and is the single most important piece of architecture in Swanage parish. Wrongly attributed to Sir Christopher Wren, after the Great Fire of 1666, it was in fact designed by Edward Jerman. Demolition appears to have taken place during 1860–61. Among the inscriptions on the walls are 'Cheapside 1670' and 'Swanage 1882'.

Southwards, being built on Durlston Head to share with Anvil Point Lighthouse the distinction of the most south-easterly buildings in the Isle of Purbeck, George Burt's major monument is Durlston Castle. He had bought the land south from Peveril Downs to Tilly Whim Quarry in 1864. La Belle Vue Restaurant, at the seaward end of La Belle Vue Road with a zig-zag path down into the rocky cliffs,

was built by George Burt in 1870. It was run in its heyday by William Hansford. In 1955, when it was owned by Philip and Ruth Burridge, the name was changed to Tilly Whim Inn. It burnt down during demolition in 1972 and has been replaced by Purbeck Heights. Weymouth architect George Crickmay balanced his 'Scottish Baronial' style of Purbeck House with 'French Riviera-style' plans for La Belle Vue Restaurant and the corbel-turreted Durlston Castle. The latter was also set on the cliffs and surrounded by innumerable tablets of stone inscribed with statistics and poetry. Building, in Purbeck stone, was carried out during 1886–87.

Three granite pillars were ordered by Sir Charles Barry for Trafalgar Square but turned out to be surplus to requirements. Burt had them brought to Swanage and inscribed: 'Durlston Head Castle, above sea 215 feet'. A sundial, on the south wall, is dated 1887. The top storey of Durlston Castle was briefly used as a Lloyd's Signal Station, from January to April 1890, and provided facilities for George Kemp on 25 March 1898. An employee of Guglielmo Marconi, he trailed a wire down the cliffs, and lay in fresh snow to listen in to his employer transmitting a radio signal from Sandbanks to The Needles, as a prelude to establishing communications with France.

Burt's Durlston inscriptions, dating from 1887 to 1891, are a marvellous pot-pourri of late Victorian outlook and scientific knowledge. Where else can you be reminded in tablets of stone that the longest day in Spitzbergen lasts three and a half months and that a ship on the horizon will have lost 66 feet 4 inches of its visual superstructure at ten miles? The latter can be put to the test from Durlston Head,

The Town Hall

Above: *Swanage Town Hall – before it arrived in the town – when it was the Mercers' Hall in Cheapside, in the City of London.*

Above and below: *Retired to the seaside, the grandiose frontage of George Burt's Town Hall, as re-erected in 1883.*

Durlston Park Estate

Right:
'Durlston Head Castle, above sea 215 ft' to quote Burt's writings at the entrance to his seaside villa.

Below:
Durlston Head (right) and Durlston Castle (centre, towards top) and the Great Globe (centre right) seen from over the sea to the south.

La Belle Vue Restaurant at Durlston in 1905.

though not to that degree of precision, and you'll have to take into account that you are 'Above sea 111 ft.' As they are gradually eroding away into history I have collected what appears to be their original entirety. Instead of their capital letters, which look ugly in print, we'll render them in upper and lower case. As for the first, David Lewer points out, Victorian wags said it was for Burt personally:

The sea is His and He made it.

No guns or sporting dogs allowed.

Caution: it is very dangerous to throw stones.

An iron coast and angry waves,
You seem to hear them rise and fall,
And roar rock thwarted in their bellowing caves,
Beneath the windy wall.

Let Prudence direct you, Temperance chasten you,
Fortitude support you;
And justice be the Guide to all your actions.

All are but parts of one stupendous whole,
Whose body Nature is, and God the soul;
Look round our World, behold the chain of Love
Combining all below and all above.
See plastic Nature working to this end,
The single atoms each to other tend,
All serv'd, all serving, nothing stands alone,
The chain holds on, and where it ends unknown.
(Pope)

God, the Creator, and Ruler of the Universe.

By the Way of the Lord were the Heavens made.
And all the host of them by the Breath of His mouth,
For He spake and it was done,
He commanded and it stood fast.
(Psalm xxxiii, 6–9)

When I consider Thy Heavens, the Moon and the Stars
which Thou hast ordained,
What is man that Thou are mindful of Him?
(Psalm viii, 3–4)

Our Nature consists in motion, perfect rest is Death.
(Pascal)

DURATION OF LONGEST DAY
at
London 16 hours 30 mins.
Hamburg 19 hours 0 mins.
Spitzbergen 3½ months.
The Poles 6 months.

CLOCK TIMES OF THE WORLD
These differ from Greenwich, 4 minutes every degree.

When 12 o'clock noon at Greenwich it is:-

EAST
at
Paris... 12.09 p.m.
Rome... 12.50 p.m.
Vienna... 1.06 p.m.
Calcutta ... 5.54 p.m.

WEST
Swanage... 11.52 a.m.
Edinburgh... 11.47 a.m.
Dublin... 11.35 a.m.
New York... 7.04 a.m.

CONVEXITY OF THE OCEAN
On looking at a vessel from ocean level we lose,
if one mile distant 0 ft. 8 ins.
five miles distant 16 ft. 7 ins.
ten miles distant 66 ft. 4 ins.
The Seas but join the nations they divide.

TIDES
These are caused by the attraction of the Sun and Moon.
The rise and fall of water being much influenced by
local conditions. Rise of tides at:

	Spring	Neap
Bristol Channel	38 ft. 0 in.	29 ft. 0 in.
Jersey	31 ft. 6 in.	23 ft. 0 in.
Southampton	13 ft. 0 in.	9 ft. 6 in.
Wexford	3 ft. 0 in.	3 ft. 6 in.

THE EARTH
The Earth is a Planet, and one of God's glorious
creations, shewing the wonders of land, air, and sea.
As seen from the nearest planet it would appear like the
beautiful 'Evening Star', having its place in the mighty
system of the worlds, as a part of the marvellous plan
of the Universe.
Equatorial Diameter about... 7,926 miles.
Equatorial Circumference... 24,900 miles.
The Surface consists of about three parts water and one
part land.
Revolves on its axis from west to east once in 23 hours,
56 minutes, 4 seconds, and moves round the Sun once
in 365 days, 5 hours, 48 minutes, 48 seconds.
The rate of the Earth's motion at the Equator is
about 1,040 miles per hour.
A Gale of Wind travels at the rate of
80 to 100 miles per hour.
The Common Black Swift flies at the rate of
200 miles per hour.
The Swallow flies at the rate of 100 miles per hour.
The Carrier Pigeon flies at the rate of 40 miles per hour.

The Earth is one of a family of eight large planets
revolving round the Sun in nearly circular paths, and
depending upon him for their light and heat.

The Sun rotates once in 25¼ days, to a point on the
Solar Equator, and is whirled round with a velocity
of 4,500 miles per hour.

THE SUN
The largest of the Heavenly bodies comprised within
the Solar System, has a diameter of about 862,000
miles, and is the source of light and heat.
Mean distance from the Earth approx. 92,000,000 miles.
Crosses the Equator twice in the year, viz., at the vernal
equinox (March 21st) and at the autumnal equinox
(September 21st), causing the varying seasons on Earth.

THE MOON
Diameter about one-fourth that of the Earth, 2,160 miles.
Mean distance from the Earth, about 238,800 miles.
Moves round the Earth once in a lunar month (28 days),
and revolves on her axis once in the same time. Hence,
very nearly the same portion of the Moon's surface is
always turned towards the Earth. The attraction of the
Sun and Moon on the Earth produces the phenomena of
the Tides, that of the Moon being about three times
as great as that of the Sun.
'Give me the ways of wandering stars to know,
The depths of Heaven above and Earth below,
Teach me the various labours of the Moon,
And whence proceed the eclipses of the Sun;
Why flowing tides prevail upon the main;
And in what dark recesses they shrink again;
What shakes the solid earth, what cause delays
The summer nights, and shortens winter days.'
(Virgil, 70–19 B.C., Translated by John Dryden,
1631–1700)

THE STARS
The distance from the Earth of the nearest fixed star,
'Alpha Centauri', visible in the Southern Hemisphere, is

computed to be 200,000 times that of the Sun Light,
which travels at the rate of about 186,000 miles in a
second, would be three-and-a-half years in reaching
the Earth from this Star.
'This World was once a fluid haze of light,
Till toward the centre set the starry tides,
And eddied into suns, that wheeling cast
The Planets.'
(Tennyson)

'O Thou Eternal One! Whose Presence bright
All space doth occupy – all motion guide;
Thou from primeval nothingness didst call,
First chaos, then existence. Lord on Thee
Eternity has its foundation! All
Spring forth from Thee! All light, joy, harmony!
Sole origin! All life, all beauty, Thine!
Thy Word created all, and doth create!
Thy splendour fills all space with rays divine!
Thou art, and wert, and shall be! Glorious! Great
Life-giving, life-sustaining Potentate!'
(Dershavin, 1743–1816)

'I made Him just and right.
Sufficient to have stood, though free to fall.'
(Milton)

'Let Nature be your teacher.'
(Wordsworth)

'Accuse not Nature! She hath done her part
Do thou but Thine!
(Milton)

'One touch of Nature makes the whole world kin.'
(Shakespeare)

COMPARATIVE SIZES

(on the same scale as this Globe, which is ten feet in diameter), mean diameters, and least and greatest
distances in miles from the Earth of the Sun, Moon and Planets. The Globe stands 136 feet above sea level.

Comparative size		Mean diameter	Least and greatest distance
The Sun would be	1090 ft. 0 in.	866,400 miles	89,900,000 to 93,000,000 miles
Jupiter	109 ft. 0 in.	86,500 miles	409,000,000 to 592,000,000 miles
Saturn	92 ft. 0 in.	73,000 miles	831,000,000 to 1,015,000,000 miles
Neptune	44 ft. 0 in.	34,800 miles	2,629,000,000 to 2,863,000,000 miles
Uranus	40 ft. 0 in.	31,900 miles	1,746,000,000 to 1,929,000,000 miles
The Earth	10 ft. 0 in.	7,918 miles	
Venus	9 ft. 3 in.	7,700 miles	24,000,000 to 159,550,000 miles
Mars	5 ft. 4 in.	4,200 miles	36,000,000 to 245,000,000 miles
Mercury	4 ft. 0 in.	3,000 miles	47,000,000 to 136,000,000 miles
The Moon	2 ft. 9 in.	2,160 miles	221,600 to 253,000 miles

A notice appears to the left of the exit which reads: 'Persons wishing to write their names will please do so on this stone only.' Some have taken up the offer and the tablets generally have not been subjected to graffiti. Westwards, the coastal path has its own inscription:

An iron coast and angry waves
You seem to hear them rise and fall.
And roar rock – thwarted in their bellowing caves

Beneath the windy wall.
Above sea 149 ft.

The Great Globe, towards the end of Durlston Head, is at the top of a flight of steps rising from the seaward information stone, which is 'Above sea 111 ft'. The forty-ton sphere, 'Above sea 136 ft', is carved in Portland stone and depicts continents, oceans and rivers. It is ten feet in diameter and was constructed for George Burt at the late John Mowlem's Greenwich works in 1887. It comprises 50 sections.

The Great Globe at Greenwich, receiving finishing touches in 1887, before removal to Durlston Head where it is seen from above the Pacific and in detail around the Caribbean.

Westwards, facing Anvil Point, the disused Tilly Whim Quarry was opened to the public as Tilly Whim Caves in 1887. Facing the Lighthouse, George Burt had an inscription carved into the vertical rock-face, 20 feet above the quarry floor:

The cloud cap'd towers
The gorgeous palaces,
The solemn temples,
The Great Globe itself.
Yea, all which it inhabit
Shall dissolve
and like the baselessness
Fabric of a vision
Leave not a rack behind.
(Shakespeare)

There had been access difficulties as visitors to Tilly Whim crossed on to a neighbouring estate. Burt solved the problem in typical fashion:

Formerly, tourists to the Tilly Whim Caves were obliged to trespass on adjacent lands, but Mr Burt came to the rescue by blasting a subterranean passage deep through the rocks, whose steep descent gives ready access to the rocks and caves. At the entrance to this subterranean passage is a granite column which now invites to the caves; formerly it 'invited' to the dungeon, for it once stood at the entrance to Pentonville! It was erected here in '1887'. Opposite, the wall buttress reads, 'Above sea 102 feet'.

The column from Pentonville Prison is in three octagonal sections. Burt also added an underground inscription to the wall of the first gallery, giving its potted history:

These caves were formed centuries ago by men making sinks and rick stones. Smuggling was also carried out here, and both were discontinued about the end of the French Wars, 1814.

Rock-falls have since closed Burt's dungeon to the public.

Left: *Tilly Whim Caves with young visitors in about 1900.*

Below: *Group called to attention, to look south from Tilly Whim Caves soon after its opening to the public in 1887, showing real grandeur before clearance of boulders.*

Ballard Down Obelisk

*Cornish granite lamp-standard from the City of London, re-erected on Ballard Down
to celebrate the abstraction of pure water from the chalk hills, with its original
gas-pipe still visible in the middle of the displaced section (left).*

The Ballard Down Obelisk, on the Swanage side of the hilltop parish boundary with Studland, has had an up and down history. The plinth is Purbeck stone and the obelisk itself is in five hexagonal sections of white Cornish granite. It was created as a lamp-standard for the City of London, and stood at Bank, outside the Church of St Mary Woolnoth on the corner of King William Street and Lombard Street. Having been removed as a highway obstruction by road-makers John Mowlem and Company it was shipped to Swanage. Two sections of the shaft, visible when strewn across the ground, had an iron gas pipe – going up the centre – and one of these, which was never reset, is propped beside the plinth.

George Burt had it erected on Ballard Down in 1892, just below the 500-feet contour, to commemorate the abstraction of pure water from the chalk aquifer, with the opening of Ulwell Reservoir at the bottom of the hill. This had enormous economic implications for the future of Swanage and would enable it to be developed into a town. The lamp-standard, however, was said to be jinxed by the ghost of a trussed-up Bronze-Age skeleton that had been dug up in the eight-foot-high round barrow on the Studland side of the landmark. Its disturbance, by Victorian antiquary John Austen, had left unstable soil that caused the obelisk to topple over. Burt had it re-erected in 1893.

Its third downfall came about during the Battle of Britain, to prevent its use as a navigation aid by German bombers, at the same time as members of the Home Guard covered the Cerne Giant hill-figure with brushwood. Re-erection did not occur until 1973, being achieved in a few hours by a summer camp of Royal Engineers from Weymouth, having resulted from the personal initiative of Bishop George Snow of Corfe Castle. He received permission from a local planning sub-committee as a 'minor departure from the coastal belt policy' which was 'subject to no adverse comment from the Department of the Environment'.

I was the first to notice the Council minute and telephone the bishop with the news. He was delighted:

It is entirely a whim on my part but I have been trying for a long time to get this obelisk put up again. It was pulled down during the war because it was a landmark. As a child I came to Swanage year after year and I came to associate a whole landscape with it. Then one day we returned after the war was over and found it on the ground.

Brigadier John Snow, who died suddenly in 1973, suggested that the Army could be persuaded to put it back on the skyline. 'It will be done by sheer manpower and block and tackle alone,' Bishop George Snow explained. 'They will carry out a reconnaissance one day and do it the next.'

Nearby, stones commemorate the Swanage Water Act of 1883, and in the town the reservoir – Swanage Water Works between Taunton Road and Purbeck Terrace Road – was built in 1886 on a truly Burtian scale and looks like a castle.

Commemorative stone, above the reservoir at Ulwell, for the Swanage Water Act of 1883.

Swanage Water Works, between Taunton Road and Purbeck Terrace Road.

Chapter 8

PIERS AND PADDLERS

Re-drawn print, being Philip Brannon's drawing of 1856 showing The Rose *at the stone quay (background, right), with the new pier and* Heather Bell *added in the foreground.*

The first wooden Swanage pier, its first in the modern sense of the word though the old stone quay was also known as a pier, was built by James Walton in 1859. The suggestion for it had come from Captain W.S. Moorsom, chief engineer of the Southampton and Dorchester Railway, as an alternative to the traditional transport of Purbeck stone in high-wheeled carts which were horse-drawn to boats at anchor in Swanage Bay. He pointed out that it would become indispensable for incoming commodities such as coal and timber. The Act of Parliament forming a Swanage Pier and Tramway Company received royal assent on 8 August 1859. Swanage Pier Act (its short title) names the original subscribers and first directors of 'The Swanage Pier Company' as John Mowlem, Edward Castleman, George Burt, Thomas Randell, George Moore Dixon, Henry Gillingham, Charles Burt, George Evans and William Tomes. It protects the interests of John Scott, Earl of Eldon, and those of other landowners, specifically Mrs Frances Serrell, the widow of Sheffield Serrell, to construct branch tramways or sidings on mineral railways passing through their properties. The tramway inland from the pier is to

'connect the stone quarries in the parishes of Langton Matravers and Swanage'.

Work at the seaward end of the project started in September 1859, on a 200-foot causeway leading to the 550-foot stretch of timbers, in a graceful arc offshore from the Grove Hotel, north-eastwards towards Peveril Point. It cost £6000 and would open in September 1861. Disputes would limit the progress of its horse-drawn tramway, 2-foot-6-inches gauge, to a matter of 375 yards along the promenade, to the bankers of cut stone awaiting shipment.

Swanage still had plenty of rough edges, viz this complaint from a visitor, published by the *Poole Pilot* newspaper on 1 March 1869:

Swanage is a charming place; its praises are in many mouths, and it cannot help rising in public favour if fair chances be afforded it. Its inaccessibility is one clog which retards its progress. The appearance of its Pier is by no means an attraction; its baldness and inconvenience discredit every inhabitant in the place. A more ugly, bone-breaking trap I have never looked at, especially for weak or invalid people. No side walk where passengers may go without fear of tripping

Left: *The two piers, with the 1879 timbers ruined in the middle distance and the 1896-built replacement behind, in a timeless view captured by Colin Graham in the 1970s.*

Above:
Stone tramway approaching the kiosk and the old pier, in a shot that has that Walter Pouncy quality, being dated to about 1895 and using for a model his favourite hirsute fisherman.

Left: *Booking Office west of the Royal Victoria Hotel, circa 1895, advertising excursions to Bournemouth and the Isle of Wight on 'Excursion Steamers* Brodick Castle *and* Lord Elgin'.

'Steamer Heather Bell *going from Swanage to Ryde'
as drawn by Emma Hardy, first wife of author
Thomas Hardy, in September 1875.*

*between the open transverse planking; an iron
tramroad projecting upwards four inches; no seat
on which tired or weak people may rest whilst waiting to
embark; no protection, not even a handrail, to prevent a
child from falling overboard and being drowned. First
impressions are, we all know, the most enduring, and
I believe many a person has condemned Swanage
immediately upon viewing this construction.*

Having failed to extend the tramway along the valley, or
to bring the national railway system from Wareham to
Swanage, George Burt decided to use the world's oldest
highway – the sea – and bought his own steamer
to run passenger services between Swanage and
Bournemouth, a distance of 7.25 miles. The *Heather Bell*
operated from 1871 to 1877. 'Bournemouth people were
originally rather jealous of my steamboat,' Burt said in
1880, continuing:

*... but in the course of a year or two they found people
said, "Is that steamboat running now? If she is, I shall
come to Bournemouth. If she is not, I shall not come."
There is no doubt about it – Bournemouth people now say
if more people could get over to Swanage they would have
more visitors, come to Bournemouth.*

That summer the steamer really discovered Swanage. It
was the year of the opening of a new pier at
Bournemouth and it was from there that most of the
visitors came. *Heather Bell* had been the pioneer steamer,
from May 1871, and *Lothair* took on the route between
Swanage and Poole, with four journeys each week,
although in 1880 she would be sold and departed
for Greece. *Telegraph* continued the service, on
Mondays and Thursdays, and *Sunshine* arrived from
Bournemouth in March. She came with 60 passengers
and most of them went on to break new ground by
setting off to visit Corfe Castle.

By the peak of the season there were so many day-
trippers arriving in Swanage that protests were made
about breaking the Sabbath. The *Telegraph* was forced to

give up the battle and returned to her home port of
Liverpool. Meanwhile, however, the Bournemouth
Steam Packet Company introduced a new steamer, the
Carham, to ply the Swanage route. Horizons opened out
both west and east when the *Princess* started to call
whilst en route between Weymouth and the Isle of
Wight. Lastly, and most importantly, there was *Florence*.
She alone could always be relied upon to return to
Swanage. She became the first to anchor beside the pier
each night and therefore came to be regarded as the
town's own steamer.

In August 1880 it was reported from Swanage that
'several hundreds are daily carried to Bournemouth and
the Isle of Wight'. Winter, however, brought the return
of the previous isolation, to the despair of the
cosmopolitan half of the town and the delight of the
less sociable.

The principal arrival in 1881 would be the *Lord
Elgin*. Big, and fast, she had been built at Stockton in
1876 and was set to steam into Swanage for the next
three decades. She was then moved sideways across the
view, into the Solent in 1911, and was the
mainstay of the Southampton–Cowes cargo service
until being withdrawn and scrapped in 1955. Local
summer services continued with a variety of smaller
vessels, such as the *Telegraph*, which plied from Poole to
Swanage on a sixpenny ticket. En route she called at
Sandbanks and established a popularity which would
see the virtually uninhabited peninsula becoming the
most expensive real estate in Britain and Europe.
Bournemouth, the flagship of the Bournemouth,
Swanage and Poole Steam Packet Company, became a
wreck on the rocks at Portland Bill in July 1886.

Brodick Castle, built at Paisley in 1877, was a
double-funnel paddle-steamer bought by the company
in 1878 to replace the ill-fated *Bournemouth*. Ironically,
Brodick Castle would go the same way, in sight of her
predecessor's grave. She had been sold to Cosens and
Company of Weymouth in 1901 and would be sold on
retirement in 1909 for use as an Argentinian
cattle-barge. The following year, whilst being towed
round Portland Bill, she took water and sank only
six miles into what should have been her
transatlantic voyage.

George Burt, in the words of John Braye in
1890, had 'transfigured' Swanage 'to such an extent that
those who knew it fifteen years ago would scarcely
recognise it, were it not for the ancient landmarks'.
Sedateness was valued by Braye and Burt who
marketed the town as a paradise for invalids, who could
recuperate in a benign climate, and benefit from
an idyllic health resort:

*The range of temperature of Swanage being so small
compared with most places, the air being so bracing
and dry, and the nearly total absence of fog, frost, and
snow should bring the little town to the notice of all
seeking a healthy spot, whether to go and settle down
indefinitely or during the colder months of the year.*

The taxi-rank of its day, with carriages along the pier approach, in about 1905.

Quietude was another virtue, though expressed with applied xenophobia, as Braye claimed that Swanage differed from the fashionable watering places in lacking 'the terrible noise occasioned by German bands or strolling nigger companies'. Such nuisances, the writer lamented, had become 'the pest' of not only English resorts but their continental counterparts.

Ventnor was one of the most successful of Victorian resorts and it came in for the envy of Swanage. All manner of statistics were thrown against this seaside competitor on the Isle of Wight, with Braye also hitting at Bournemouth for good measure, after dealing first with the competition from Ventnor:

One great disadvantage is that it is overrun with invalids of every description, which is very depressing. Bournemouth, though on the opposite side to Swanage, is in no way so good a residence for invalids. The air is much too relaxing, and after staying there a short time the invalid feels this. There is a want of the tonic air so conspicuous in Swanage. I would also mention the comparative warmness of the Swanage minimum temperature, throughout the year, as compared with Bournemouth, and hence of course the smallness of range at Swanage. Many of the invalids from Bournemouth will probably migrate over to Swanage as time rolls on.

This popularity, and continuing adverse comment on the shambolic mixture of commercial activity competing for limited facilities, led to Swanage Pier Company deciding to build a second pier, as a extension from the landward end of the first structure. Designed by R. St George Moore, with the civil engineer being Alfred Thorne of Westminster, it was to be 642 feet long, with an average width of 28 feet. Work started in November 1895 and would cost £10 000. Imported green-heart timber, rather than the usual cast iron, was used for its 170 piles, and promised resistance to worm and decay. Top-decking was in pitch pine.

Work was still in progress when the *Lord Elgin* became its first steamer to arrive, on May Day in 1896, and the final pile was driven into the seabed on 26 July 1896. Brisk business ensued, reaching 10 000 arrivals from paddle-steamers in 1897. They paid 1s.6d. for a return ticket from Bournemouth; of which Swanage Pier Company took a penny royalty. A dozen steamers put in regular appearances. The most adventurous made the 62-mile trip to Cherbourg. No Sunday sailings took place until 1929.

Contemporary with *Brodick Castle*, the *Empress* was Thames-built in 1879, being bought brand-new by Cosens and Company of Weymouth. This single-funnelled oscillating engine vessel would go on to have the longest career of all the

Above: *Entrance to the pier in its Edwardian heyday.*

Below: *Visitors arriving at the new pier, from the paddle-steamer* Brodick Castle *in 1906.*

paddle-steamers in local waters. She was first seen off Swanage in 1880 and went on to survive two world wars. Then she became a star, in 1946, in David Lean's classic film of Charles Dickens' *Great Expectations*. Her end was then conventional; to the breaker's yard, when the first replacements arrived for the expected leisure revival in 1955. Her engine was spared – being the last of its type – and is preserved in Southampton Maritime Museum.

Overlapping most of her career was the *Monarch*, a double-funnelled paddle-steamer operated by Cosens. She was assigned to the Bournemouth-Swanage service for more than half a century, from 1880 to 1950, and was then broken up.

The original pier, to the south-east of the new one, was in visible decay throughout the 20th century. Before the First World War it was used for ancillary purposes, such as coaling steamers, and providing overnight berths for *Majestic* and *Monarch*. Such facilities deteriorated beyond repair. Appropriately, it became a diving platform for the final users, Swanage Swimming Club. Thereafter it decayed into a double line of intermittent stumps.

Such a future also seemed to await the second Swanage pier. Its decay-resistant timbers proved to be excellent eating for a wood-boring marine crustacean of the Limnoria genus, the gribble, which devoured the inter-tidal sections. The damage was arrested but not repaired by concrete encasement in 1927. Then came the Second World War, with the Sappers inflicting deliberate destruction, removing the landward end of both piers by explosives, to deprive German invaders of port facilities.

There would be a post-war revival, starting after the Government-paid restitution of war damage in 1948, and for a while things looked remarkably buoyant, until the unprecedented expansion of the holiday trade took unexpected turns with the younger clientele discovering holiday camps and aviation widening the overseas horizon. *Swanage Queen* carried the town's name from Weymouth to Lulworth and her home waters. The last regular paddle-steamer service would cease in 1964 and *Empress* became the last Weymouth-based steamer to use the pier, on 24 September 1966.

Non-appearance of steamers made news in 1965, almost as if cuckoos and swallows were no longer going to return:

Consul, Britain's oldest paddle-steamer has ploughed the seas from Weymouth to Bournemouth since 1897. But she has been losing money for the past two years and her owners, Cosens and Co, are to lay her up at Weymouth. This year, for the first time in living memory, there will be no paddle-steamer trips to Lulworth Cove.

Subsequently, the Paddle Steamer Preservation Society revived the experience, with nostalgic returns of the Clyde-based *Waverley*. She would become the last ocean-going paddle-steamer and was a relative youngster, being a post-war Government-provided replacement for her namesake which was lost in the Dunkirk evacuation of May 1940.

The pier nearly became absorbed into a yacht marina, under plans by Durrant Developments in 1987, but emerged from that threat and subsequent dereliction into a new age of Heritage Lottery Fund grants. Nothing seemed that certain in 1992, when the receivers of Durrant Developments (Swanage Yacht Haven) Limited sold the pier to Purbeck District Council, for the token sum of £1.

Since 1994 its statutory management authority, the Swanage Pier Company, has held joint meetings with Swanage Pier Trust, acting as its charity wing. Legally it is designated as a harbour, under the Harbours Act of 1964. Restoration of the stonework of the pier approach cost £75 000. Gribbled piles have been replaced at £6000 a time. The decking has been completely replaced. Embellishments have given back Victorian era character, such as cast-iron railings and lamp standards, with distinctive flourishes. A small landing stage has been tucked under the seaward extremity. On top there is a wind-shelter. By 2001 a total of £1.1 million had been spent on rescuing the Grade-II listed structure.

'It needs the best commercial income it can get,' says Purbeck District Council Chief Executive Paul Croft, who acts as Secretary for Swanage Pier Company:

Everything made on the pier is ploughed back into its maintenance. At the moment there is not enough to put aside proper provision for further restoration. We have to face the fact that it is never going to be a profit maker.

The Victorians provided the piers and the Edwardians followed with the promenade. This topped the recently constructed sea wall northwards beside the sands. A foundation stone, laid by Sir John Mowlem Burt on 25 February 1904, survives close to the Mowlem Theatre though its inscription is no longer legible. The building was done by Sir John's family firm and completion was achieved in June 1905.

The other change to the appearance of seaside Swanage during the 20th century was the building of groynes, extending seawards at 90 degrees from the beach, along two-thirds of a mile from The Mowlem to the Grand Hotel. The series of wooden barriers date from 1926. They have successfully stemmed the erosive effects of tidal drift but were initially resisted and resented for spoiling the open sweep of the sands. Inshore, yachts are now the most familiar vessels, with tankers and container-ships as the passing traffic along the horizon.

Above: *Looking westwards from the pier head, as arrivals head towards the town, before 1905.*

Below: Lord Elgin *operated on the Bournemouth–Swanage run from 1881 until 1911, and is seen reversing into Swanage bay, with Ballard Point in the background.*

Above: *Two paddle-steamers and two piers, with the 1859-structure still relatively intact in the foreground, seen in the 1930s.*

Below: Swanage Queen, *from Weymouth, was among the last of the regular callers and is seen coming into Swanage in July 1961.*

Chapter 9

SHIPWRECKS AND LIFEBOATS

Shipwreck salvage, of lead ingots, being raised from the wreck of the Fanny.

One of the earliest recorded instances of shipwrecks off the British Isles is documented in the *Anglo-Saxon Chronicle* for 877. The previous year, after months of fighting, the West Saxons bribed the Danes, who had sailed into Wareham, to negotiate a truce. Saxon silver bought the return of hostages and the Danes gave King Alfred their solemn oath 'on the holy ring' that they would leave Wessex. The enemy longships departed from Wareham but did not return home. Instead they turned the other way in the English Channel and went on to occupy Exeter.

The *Anglo-Saxon Chronicle* is ambiguous about the cause of the subsequent shipwrecks. There are five extant versions of the manuscript. Three put the failure of Danish reinforcements to arrive in Exeter down to a gale, saying they 'encountered a great storm at sea, and 120 ships were lost at Swanage'. The other two versions say they 'encountered a great mist at sea, and 120 ships were lost at Swanage'. In all probability it was a combination of foul weather with disorientation in thick fog being followed by

strong winds. The failure of the full Danish force to reach Exeter caused the remainder to accede to Alfred's demands and quit the city, leaving Devon for Gloucester, which was in Mercian territory.

The next vessel half-known to have been lost off Swanage was a Spanish vessel in 1425, its name not recorded, which is not documented in English records but has left a mention in Madrid.

The *Neptune*, a Swanage stone-boat, 'bulged' in February 1791. This is the nautical term for a boat's sides splitting open. Finding herself in difficulties she beached in the shallow waters of Poole Harbour and was abandoned.

Bound for London, from south Wales, the *Fanny* sank half a mile east of Peveril Point, in January 1793. She was carrying a cargo of lead in 200cwt ingots. Some of these were raised and brought ashore, in 1979, by Eddie Bennett. Although there was unlikely to be a claimant, after a couple of centuries, the Receiver of Wrecks impounded the salvaged metal for a year and a day, this being the statutory period that has to elapse before the finder becomes keeper.

Right: *Peveril Point and its Coastguard lookout, with naval ratings and its alarm gun (the mortar in front of the hut).*

Above: *One of the town's earliest photographs, showing the decorated arch across the High Street for Miss E.M. Scott, who funded the first Purbeck lifeboat, which was brought by rail to Wareham and road to Swanage for launching, after which it was stationed at Kimmeridge. On the right of the arch is Purbeck House, with suspended anchor, giving 'Thanks' to E.M.S. on 21 November 1866.*

Below: *Coastguard lookout on Peveril Point, looking southwards across Durlston Bay to Durlston Head, in about 1910.*

The Exeter schooner *Sisters* was wrecked on the ledges off Peveril Point in November 1827 with the loss of seven of her crew. One man was rescued, being dragged ashore at great risk to themselves by Swanage Coast Guards and boatmen who were rewarded by the newly-formed Royal National Institution for the Preservation of Lives from Shipwreck, which had been founded by Sir William Hillary in 1824.

The French brig *Jean-Marie* was wrecked on Peveril Point in April 1839. Lieutenant (later Vice-Admiral) George Davies of the Royal Navy, the officer commanding Swanage Coast Guard, led a daring rescue which also involved the Revenue cutter *Tartar*. All eight crewmen were saved and several silver medals were awarded to the rescuers.

A local committee was formed in Swanage in 1874 to obtain a lifeboat for the town. It had Mr (later Sir) J.C. Robinson as its patron, George Burt as president, Mr (later Sir) Reginald Palgrave as Vice-President, Richard Haynes (of Magnolia House), John Haysom (Purbeck Hotel), George Horlock (postmaster), William Trayte (Robinson's steward) and James Pope (banker). They were encouraged by Miss Julia Colson, the daughter of the late vicar, who was the local organiser of the Shipwrecked Mariners' Society.

Meanwhile the inauspiciously-named *Wild Wave*, an Exeter brigantine, came to grief on Peveril Point on 23 January 1875. She balanced on one of the outer ledges, pounded by a ferocious sea that prevented two gigs attempting a rescue. A rope was fired by rocket from the shore but the line was lost as the stricken vessel lurched. Further attempts were rendered futile by a combination of darkness and the dire conditions. To everyone's surprise, however, there was still a precariously wedged brigantine on the ledge at dawn. Six crewmen were still visible, and audible, as they screamed for help. This time the gig had a successful run, coming alongside, though being bounced and bumped by the waves. All the crew jumped for their lives with only moments to spare. Then, just as the rescue had been effected, their vessel slipped for the last time in what would have been a death roll from the rocks to the seabed. The rescue was seen as a miracle and was used to make the case for a lifeboat.

The decision to accede to the petitions from Swanage was agreed by the London-based committee of the Royal National Lifeboat Institution on 4 March 1875. The timing was convenient as it coincided with unplaced funds, from a bequest by Miss Margaret Ryder Wilde, passed on by her nephew Samuel J. Wilde of Serjeant's Inn, with the request from his aunt that the new lifeboat should be named *Charlotte Mary* in memory of her two sisters.

The Earl of Eldon gave a plot of foreshore at the south-east corner of Swanage Bay. This was protected from the prevailing winds by Peveril Downs and from the south-easterlies by Peveril Point which projected seawards about 250 yards to the east. The Lifeboat House cost £350 and its slipway £175. It and the house were in service in a matter of months, being declared open on 16 September 1875, with the naming of *Charlotte Mary* by Mrs Samuel Wilde. Her coxswain was William Masters who was at that time providing lodgings to author Thomas Hardy and his wife Emma in West End Cottage. He would be immortalised as Captain Flower in the *Hand of Ethelberta* and Mrs Masters has a mention in the poem on *The Lodging House Fuchsias*, penned as an eulogy for Emma.

Homeward bound, with French products for the Paris Exhibition in New York, the famous old American frigate USS *Constitution* ran aground between Ballard Point, then known as Ballard Head, and Old Harry Rocks, 'in the haze and mist of the night' on 17 January 1879. She immediately began firing her guns to announce her plight. Guns, ammunition, chains, cables and other heavy items were removed to lighten the old three-masted sailing vessel in the cold light of the morning. Five steamers then spent several hours trying to pull her clear. Eventually a Government tug arrived, from Southampton, and this additional assistance enabled them to release the *Constitution*. She was towed to Portsmouth, where only minor damage was found, and resumed her Transatlantic voyage. She was reckoned to have enjoyed a miracle escape.

Less fortunate, only a week later, was the 500-ton Norwegian schooner *Annie Margretta*, coincidentally attempting the same route. She came ashore only a few hundred yards away from the *Constitution's* coastal encounter.

The vessel was in difficulty in the early hours of 24 January 1879 but for hours the Swanage Lifeboat found it impossible to respond, being unable to launch down the Peveril slipway against a heavy sea being driven directly inshore by an easterly gale. That problem caused the Lifeboat Institution to build a groyne to hold back the waves. The remains of the *Annie Margretta* were sold at auction, as a total wreck, for £45.

Portland had Dorset's first and only lighthouses until 1880 when Trinity House started work on defining the almost equally treacherous south-eastern extremity of the Dorset coast. The twin headlands of Anvil Point and Durlston Head were regarded as more in need of a light than the southern tip of the Isle of Purbeck at St Alban's Head, though it was accepted that the latter also represented a major hazard. Lighthouse Road was constructed as a mile-long access to Anvil Point, southwards from Sunnydale Road on the outskirts of Swanage, and the lighthouse was completed in 1882, on the slope overlooking Tilly Whim Caves.

*Purbeck's treacherous coast, presenting a wall of vertical stone, sketched by
Sir James Pelie on 18 August 1882, showing 'Tilly Whim and the new
Light-House' – and in a photograph from the same spot, taken in 1900.*

Anvil Point

Right: *Squat tower of the lighthouse on Anvil Point which may lack stature but makes up for it in terms of position.*

Below: *Seen from seawards, looking north-east, Anvil Point Lighthouse with speed trial marker (right) and opening into Tilly Whim Caves (far right).*

Below: *Aerial view of Anvil Point and the lighthouse, from the south-west, looking towards Durlston Castle (right).*

The Olive Branch *wrecked and immobilised by icing, January 1895, to the east of the stone quay at Swanage, with the Mowlem Institute glimpsed in the background (left).*

The 1230-ton Liverpool sailing ship *Alexandrovna* was disabled by a hurricane in the English Channel in the early hours of Saturday 29 April 1882. As the winds abated it was realised that the vessel was missing. During the afternoon, however, she was seen drifting towards the newly operational lighthouse on Anvil Point, with her topsails in ribbons and just a single stay-sail set. There was still a heavy sea running offshore and breaking into white-water inshore. No crew were seen. In minutes 'the fated ship was among the broken billows which covered the sea with foam for hundreds of yards from the rocks'. Witnesses realised the vessel was on a collision course with the Ragged Rocks below the perpendicular stone cliffs half a mile west of Round Down. The prospective rescuers ran from the point to the spot, but in the ten minutes they took to arrive she had been dashed to pieces, and nothing could be seen of her crew of 77. It was soon realised that all had been lost as bodies were found 'jammed in among the rocks, or floating in the waters of the Channel, most of them bearing marks of frightful injuries – inflicted, it is to be hoped, after death.'

A macabre sequel took place the following Thursday when the pleasure steamer *Empress* brought a large party of visitors from Bournemouth and Swanage, around Durlston Head, 'to see the remnants of the sad wreck' which included two substantial sections of the ship. They saw more than 'immense quantities of wreck' and watched as a naked body was recovered with a lifebuoy in its arms. Others were picked up 'much bruised and disfigured'.

Charles Edmund Robinson, writing at Newton Manor, provides the contemporary account of the effects of the hurricane, in a reminder to us that severe weather happenings are not just a recent occurrence:

The phenomenal violence of the gale may be judged from the fact that sea-salt is recorded to have been blown by it more than a hundred miles inland; and that it completely stripped all the trees in exposed situations on the coast of their young green leaves, which the spring had just brought out. The elms at Swanage were not covered with leaf again until past midsummer.

Christmas turned into tragedy on Boxing Day in 1886 for the six crewmen of the brigantine *Forest Queen*. She was en route down the Channel, from Antwerp, with a cargo of phosphate bound for Silloth in Cumbria. She was doubly unlucky in failing to round the extremity of the headland forming the south-eastern corner of the Isle of Purbeck and was then driven into the rocky cleft between Anvil Point and Durlston Head. The crew decided to abandon ship but the gale-force wind, from the south east, piled up a tremendous sea which pounded into the gully beneath Tilly Whim Caves. They managed to lower the ship's boat but drowned as it was washed inshore and dashed to pieces.

Rowing practice for the crew of **Herbert Sturmey**, *the Swanage Lifeboat, with Walter Masters at the prow in 1924.*

Right: *The Mersey-class* Robert Charles Brown *required an extended Lifeboat House in 1991.*

Thomas Markby, *the Swanage Lifeboat, on the ramped slipway at Peveril Point.*

The second Swanage lifeboat, larger than *Charlotte Mary*, was the 37-foot *William Erle*. She had twelve oars and was named in December 1890 by her donor, Lady Erle, in memory of her late husband, Chief Justice Sir William Erle. The vessel was rejected by the crew, who claimed she was unstable, and would be replaced by a second *William Erle* in 1893.

Her first rescue attempt, into a blizzard on 12 January 1895, had to be called off when the coxswain, William Brown, was swept to his death off Old Harry Rocks. The turbulent and confused sea nearly claimed the lifeboat as well. It was a sad start for the second *William Erle* but she handled well and would carry out many successful rescues before retiring through old age in 1914. David Hibbs, who lived to the north of the Mowlem in the White House, also retired, after having been a lifeboatman since 1893.

The difficult years of European conflict would be tackled by the self-righting *Zaida* which had come secondhand from Carrickfergus. The First World War brought the menace of German U-boats and a growing toll of shipping torpedoed in the western sectors of the English Channel. The biggest and closest victim to be sunk within sight of Swanage was the 4383-ton merchant vessel *Kyarra*, a mile and a half off Durlston Head, in a massive explosion on 5 May 1918. Nine crewmen were killed. The ship was relatively modern, having been built on the Clyde in 1903, and was owned by the Australian United Steamship Company. She had just begun what should have been a return journey to Sydney.

The wreck sits upright on the sea-bed and still stands to 30 feet, in 100 feet of water, and was one of the first to be discovered after the advent of lightweight leisure diving in the 1960s. Her finder was a lady from London and the wreck would be bought by her diving club. She has since claimed a further life. Martin Pilcher, a 44-year-old marine artist and photographer drowned in a diving mishap when he attempted an exploration inside the ship in 1992.

Zaida, the wartime Swanage lifeboat, was replaced by *Herbert Sturmey* in a presentation on 12 October 1918. She was named for the deceased benefactor. Also self-righting, she would be among the last of the sailing lifeboats to be constructed, and would continue in service until 1928.

At 40 feet in length, the next Swanage lifeboat was a little longer than her predecessor, and the first to have an engine. Watched by just about the whole town, from Peveril Point, *Thomas Markby* was launched down a reconstructed slipway on 7 July 1928. *Thomas Markby* survived her longest and most demanding call-out on 4 July 1937, when she spent 12 hours in 70-mph minds, towing the yacht *Panorama* across Lyme Bay to safety in Weymouth.

Manned by 11 members of the Royal Navy Volunteer Reserve and returning empty from St Valery, where she had been helping evacuate remnants of the British and French armies, HMS *Abel Tasman* hit a German mine in the Swash Channel entrance to Poole Harbour on 13 June 1940. She was blown to pieces, killing all on board, and one crewman, 20-year-old Ordinary Seaman E.J.H. Gosling, is buried in Swanage Cemetery at Washpond Lane.

Somewhat to the surprise of its crew, the Swanage lifeboat *Thomas Markby* survived the Second World War and its interminable searches for shot-down pilots and the victims of mines and torpedoes, in waters under the eye of the Luftwaffe.

A post-war wreck, that of the submarine HMS *Safari*, lies off Anvil Point and would claim the life of Poole lifeboatman Pete Benson in July 1992, whose secondhand buoyancy gear failed him on a dive.

On retirement in 1949 Swanage lifeboat *Thomas Markby* was replaced by a Watson-class vessel, 41 feet long with 35-horsepower engines, which was named with the initials *R.L.P.* for R.L. Pugh from Kensington.

Centenary year for the Swanage lifeboat, 1975, saw the arrival of its eighth boat. This was the Rother-class *J. Reginald Corah*. The 38-foot vessel was named for a Leicester industrialist who had died in 1955. Llew Hardy, the onshore co-ordinator for rescues, was asked how he regarded the romantic side of the job. 'There's nothing glamorous about putting out to sea in bad weather to search half the night for a missing boat,' he told the reporter.

In October 1976 the *J. Reginald Corah* was launched into conditions described as 'the worst for over 30 years' to save the lives of two Frenchmen in a yacht. The Lifeboat Institution's bronze medal for gallantry would be awarded to Swanage boatmen Ron Hardy and Victor Marsh. The lifeboat had been damaged in the rescue and might have been lost but for the skill of their manoeuvring. As the boat was being pounded by violent waves, Mr Marsh risked his life in the attempted removal of a rope, which had wrapped around the propeller. Crew members Chris Haw, George Bishop, Eric Dorey, Pete Hardy and Ian Marsh received certificates in recognition of their part in the rescue. It started when the Russian trawler *Topaz* spotted the French yacht in difficulties and took her in tow. The trawler then radioed Portland Coastguard to take over the rescue. The Swanage lifeboat was mobilised to meet the trawler off Peveril Point but language difficulties prevented a smooth transfer. By that time, in the storm-force-ten winds of 60 miles per hour, there was a rise and fall of 20 feet between the peaks and troughs of the waves. Lines were eventually secured and the first Frenchman descended a rope-ladder to jump aboard the lifeboat. It then took several approaches of the *J. Reginald Corah* before the second yachtsman had enough confidence to leap aboard the heaving boat. His rescuers then picked up the yacht's towrope but in doing so it fouled the lifeboat's rudder and propeller. The yacht had to be cut clear. Victor Marsh

*Storm damage of April 1988 with wreckage of fishing boat SU 301 beached and
PE 306 reduced to pieces offshore, being seen with the Clock Tower in the background.*

then tried to clear the propeller with a freeing tool but this procedure was impossible with the boat rolling so violently. Waves were smashing through the scuttle and over the stern.

Coxswain Ron Hardy decided to make for Swanage on only one engine. He put a member of his crew on the yacht with a makeshift drogue made of old ropes. Because of the desperate conditions, returning to Swanage was an impossibility, and the two boats had to head north for the calmer waters of Poole Harbour. The drogue successfully controlled the yacht except as they crossed the shallow sands of the Bar off Shell Bay. It required the efforts of a diver at Poole Quay to clear the entangled propeller. There had been damage to the boat but the Lifeboat Institution report concluded that this could have been 'much more serious but for Coxswain Hardy's superb seamanship'. It added that without Victor Marsh's efforts to clear it, and particularly 'his prudent checking of the other propeller shaft, the lifeboat could easily have been left in the storm without power.'

The Lifeboat House was extended in 1991 and its slipway replaced. This was for its Mersey-class lifeboat *Robert Charles Brown*. The brand-new state-of-the-art vessel had the distinction of being the first to be named for a local stalwart of the service – a long-standing coxswain – rather than a wealthy benefactor. The cost of £350 000 had been raised by the local appeals group of the Royal National Lifeboat Institution. Capable of 16.5 knots, with a reinforced resin hull, she carried a minimum crew of five and had a turn-out time of seven minutes. As well as satellite navigation, radar and depth-sounding equipment she carried a VHF direction finder to home in on the radio signal of a vessel in distress.

Seldom do gales cause more destruction on land than at sea but the exception came on Thursday 25 January 1990. With westerly winds recorded at 110 mph at Land's End and 105 mph on Dartmoor in the middle of the morning, the most serious of the late-20th-century hurricanes gusted across the West Country. It had lost none of its ferocity on arrival in Swanage. As well as the usual gale-born debris of branches, tiles and fencing, whole sections of roofs were ripped off, and the entire inflatable sports hall at the town's Harrow International Language and Sports Centre took to the sky. Its giant dome, complete with equipment, ended up in nearby tennis courts. The avenue of trees on the school's approach road was uprooted, along with many single specimens throughout the town.

There was also tragedy. Retired printer John Green of Holmes Road, Swanage, who was walking along Station Road, was swept off his feet by a freak gust. He spun in the air and landed on his head, fracturing his skull, and would die that night in Poole General Hospital. He was born in 1911.

In 1993 a second inshore boat was taken on to cope with an increasing volume of shoreline misadventures on the part of swimmers and surfers. Chris Haw was the coxswain of the *Robert Charles Brown* until July 2000.

As for Swanage and the sea, in its more manageable moods, the prominent white-painted steel poles at Anvil Point and a similar pair a mile to the west on the cliffs south of Verney Farm, were erected for speed calculations in naval trials.

Early Victorian print of Shep's Hollow, looking across the bay to the Isle of Wight.

Chapter 10
HEALTH AND HOSPITALS

The town was well served by its doctors with the Delamotte family covering most of the 19th century and being followed by Admiralty surgeon Llewelyn Baiss who lived at Harberton in Rempstone Road. Swanage Cottage Hospital in Queen's Road, a neat Victorian building, was erected as a memorial to George and Elizabeth Burt by their surviving children, daughters Emma Burt and Annie Burt, and sons John Mowlem Burt and George Burt junr. Its name is set into the frontage in Roman-style mosaic letters of tesserae cubes. The building was declared open by the Bishop of Salisbury on 26 February 1895 and had 16 public beds and two private wards. Stone donation boxes flank the entrance which opens into an imposing foyer with a plaque to philanthropic Emma Rose Burt who had been the secretary to the town's previous hospital in improvised buildings in the High Street. She would run Swanage Cottage Hospital until her death in 1911.

Subsequent supporters, grouping as the League of Friends, saw off closure threats in the 1970s and raised considerable sums to supplement National Health Service funding. In the first phase of improvements, in collaboration with the Lions Club, they raised £390 000 of the £485 000 cost. The result of this and an unfolding £1 million scheme has been the complete revamping of in-patient facilities plus provision of the Stanley Purser wing and Walter de Jersey day area. Old wards were replaced by 15 in-patient beds and places. Three single rooms included one devoted to long-term palliative care. New physiotherapy, audiology and occupational therapy facilities were provided. The accident unit copes with minor injuries and has seen a staggering rise in the number of casualties, doubling from 3500 in 1995 to 7000 in 1999, which has to be seen in the light of the numbers coming to the town for leisure and pleasure. It would otherwise amount to the alarming average of a mishap to every person in its catchment area every other year.

Maggie Hardy, the wife of Merchant Navy Captain Neil Hardy of the Peninsula and Orient Line, has been the manager of the expanded Swanage Hospital since 1992.

During and after the First World War, before the extended reach of Goring's Luftwaffe, Swanage was regarded as the ideal place for recuperating military casualties. The town had an RAF hospital and a Red Cross hospital. It was also provided with Swanage Children's Hospital, in the former Palgrave family home at Hill Side, in Peveril Road. On its opening day, 31 October 1919, Colonel John Balguy from Lower Bockhampton at Stinsford brought a former parishioner from there – and sometime Swanage resident – namely the author Thomas Hardy. They were joined by Lady Ilchester from Melbury House and Dr Charles John Ridgeway, the Bishop of Salisbury, who performed a service of dedication.

Swanage Hospital

Pictures top and bottom: *Maggie Hardy (top, left) and members of her staff in Swanage Hospital, representing the National Health Service and photographed by Rodney Legg in 2000.*

Left: *Reminder of philanthropic private provision, when the Burt family provided the facilities and patients were asked for donations, in 1895.*

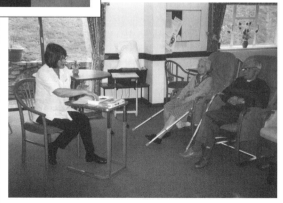

Chapter 11
CHURCHES AND CEMETERIES

The Anglican Parish Church, dedicated to St Mary, stands below the mill-pond in the heart of Old Swanage, with only the 14th-century tower surviving from the medieval building. Its Victorian and Edwardian rebuildings were almost total. The former, during 1859–60, renewed the nave, south transept and stair-turret. Its architect was Thomas Henry Wyatt (1807–80) whose major works include the Liverpool Exchange, Wilton Church, Knightsbridge Barracks, and the Athenaeum extensions. As consultant architect to the Incorporated Church Building Society and Salisbury Diocesan society, he designed or restored a total of more than 150 churches. His idiom at Swanage was 13th-century Gothic. It was consecrated by the Bishop of Salisbury in July 1860:

His lordship preached a sermon from 2 Chronicles, xviiii, 16. The collection amounted to £239, including £100 from Mr Mowlem; £52 from Mr Hunt, of Godlingston Farm; and £50 from Mr White, churchwarden.

This work and a whole raft of community projects was instigated by 'building rector' Revd Duncan Travers who was the incumbent from 1854 to 1887. He had already set about acquiring land off Northbrook Road, in 1855, for a new cemetery. Then, having rebuilt St Mary's, he added a couple of large rooms to Swanwic House, which was then the rectory, in 1860. He trebled the size of the National School, converted a coach-house into the Parish Room, extended Herston Schools, and gave the hamlet its own church. He later installed 'hot water apparatus' and advised the Earl of Eldon on the restoration of the Parish Church at Worth Matravers.

The northwards expansion of St Mary's in 1907–08 added what is in effect a second church running parallel to the Victorian building and stretching further west than the original tower.

Perpendicular styles from the 15th century were the choice of architects James E. Clifton and Edmund A. Robinson who were both from Swanage. Their work has its dedication stone on the north-east outside corner, dated 10 October 1907, which was laid by Winifred Parsons, daughter of rector Revd W.H. Parsons. The builders, also from the town, were H. and J. Hardy. Their principal mason was Isaac Edmonds.

During the rebuilding an ancient consecration cross was discovered. It was 'built into the north wall of the new nave on the inside'. The work also uncovered other earlier features, including 13th-century moulded fragments, two 14th-century coffin-lids, and the remains of a couple of 15th-century cusped window-heads.

The Congregational Chapel, on the north side of the High Street near its rounded corner with Church Hill, carries stones proclaiming 'Built 1705' and 'Rebuilt 1837'. Its rebuilding was total, by George Gollop of Poole, into the solid, plain, upright lines of Victorian perpendicular architecture. The 1837 chapel was later converted to a schoolroom and a new church added on the east side, with a memorial to its early-19th-century deacon, Samuel Marsh, who died in 1841.

The foundation stone for the new church 'was laid by Stephen Collins, son of the late Mr William Collins, for many years a deacon of this church, August 22nd 1900'. The north wall was blown out, destroying the organ, by a German bomb in 1943. It is now the United Reformed Church.

Similar stones also survive for the foundation of the Wesleyan Chapel – 'built 1827, enlarged 1842' – incorporated in the later Methodist Church on the south side of High Street.

Picture inset: *St Mary's Parish Church, as it looked from the south-east, engraved by W.A. Miles in 1826.*

St Mary's

Left: *Pews and galleries in the Parish Church, sketched by Julia Colson, shortly before its rebuilding in 1859.*

Below: *Town view of St Mary's Church, northwards down Church Hill from the High Street, c.1890.*

Inset opposite page: *Rustic view of St Mary's Church, looking north-eastwards from pastures beside the High Street in about 1890, with a haystack beside the stone wall (bottom left).*

Above: *Mill Pond Farm and the tower of St Mary's Church from the south-west, c.1900.*

The parish's first detached cemetery, immediately across the road from the south-east corner of St Mary's Church, was consecrated on 12 October 1826. Its slope has been partially cleared, including the removal of the memorial to its founder, Revd Thomas Oldfeld Bartlett, in the process of turning it into a strip of wooded parkland. Robert Burt's family vault has survived at the top end. An exemplar of the new Victorian values appears on the memorial to 85-year-old Nathan Chinchen who died on 16 May 1840. Even then they may have had to rebut suggestions of an oriental connection, with the stone referring to 'a name well-known in this vicinity in his generation'. It continues:

His beloved remains are deposited in a vault in the burying ground adjacent, where he was placed in the sure and certain hope that when those that sleep in the dust of the Earth shall awake, he will rise clothed in his redeemer's righteousness to everlasting life.

An anonymous 22-year-old, from 1844, has gone from blessed affliction 'to the grave where none pardon can win' which sounds much like a continuation of childhood ordeals: 'O merciful Father I welcome the rod, since by it I am brought to a sense of my sin.'

The main Victorian cemetery, opened in 1856, covers an acre and a half on the north side of The Brook and railway, west of the southern end of Northbrook Road and the bland late-20th-century architecture of Gilbert Court. John Mowlem's tomb rises above the rest. It rises vertically and is then stepped, into a pyramid of matching blue Guernsey granite, which reaches 20 feet above the grass.

'MDCCCLXIX' on the foundation stone of St Mark's Church in Bell Street, Herston, coincided with the demise of its architect, John Hicks of Dorchester, who died on 12 February 1869. This simple Anglican building has a steeply-pitched roof with a bell turret. It is of more interest for the draughtsmanship of its plans rather than the architecture.

The work was brought to a conclusion by George Crickmay of Weymouth, who almost certainly delegated the task to his assistant, the novelist Thomas Hardy. As a teenager, Hardy had been Hicks' pupil, from 1856 to 1862, and was employed by him again at the end of the decade, from 1867. On Hicks' death, Crickmay took on

Hardy specifically to finish off the church projects that he had inherited from Hicks' practice.

Shortage of money delayed completion, and consecration did not take place until 25 April 1872; this being St Mark's Day. The master mason was Felix G. Fooks of Herston. Contemporary accounts describe it as 'a plain Early English village church, inexpensive' – £1400, actually – 'but nevertheless pretty and of effective design'. Its oldest feature is secondhand, being an octagonal 1663-dated Purbeck stone font from St Mary's Parish Church. Herston Church was extended, at the south-west corner, in the 1970s.

The Methodist Church, set back from the High Street on the south side, about 200 yards south east of St Mary's Church, is the best Victorian Gothic in town. It was built in 1886 and rises into a tower topped by a steeple. The main church has its commemorative stones set near ground-level at the corners. An earlier foundation stone, for its predecessor Wesleyan Chapel, is re-set in the east wall of the present car park. The replacement stones document its wealthy benefactors. On the east side: 'This stone was laid by G. Burt Esq, JP, Aug 14th 1885... This stone was laid by G.E. Robinson Esq, Aug 14th 1885.' On the west side: 'This stone was laid by Mrs Jobson of London. Relict of the Rev. F. Jobson DD, Aug 14th 1885... This stone was laid by Sir W.M. Arthur KCMG, MP, Aug 14th 1885.'

George Burt puts in an appearance, literally, carved over the entrance, together with Wesleyan minister Revd George Terry. Their faces are life-size and both bearded but set high, on each side of the main window, where they are not immediately noticeable. Inside, lengthy inscriptions commemorate Terry and this 'so-called Wesley Memorial Church' and record that George Burt added the spire 'in affectionate memory of his grandmother, Mary Burt'. The earlier Burts have their memorials recording that Mary, who died aged 85 on 13 March 1826, had half a century before 'walked to Salisbury and brought the Revd John Wesley on his first visit to Swanage'. Matching in style, the Wesley Centenary Hall and Sunday School were added on the east side of the church in 1907. Here stand a line of dedication stones including one to 'Mr Moses Manwell, aged 90. Local Preacher 60 years.'

St Mary's

Above: *St Mary's Church, from the north-east, after its Edwardian extensions.*

Left: *The original churchyard extension, across the road from St Mary's Parish Church, dominated by the broken column erected over Robert Burt's grave in 1847.*

Below: *St Mary's Choir, with Revd William Henry Parsons, the rector from 1905 to 1908.*

Right: *Annual summer outing for the Congregational Church Choir, across the hill to Studland, in 1895.*

Below: *Swanage history is often conveniently writ in the stone – such as these inscriptions telling us the Congregational Chapel was 'Built 1705, Rebuilt 1837'.*

Below: *The United Reformed Church, in the High Street, extending eastwards from the earlier Congregational Chapel.*

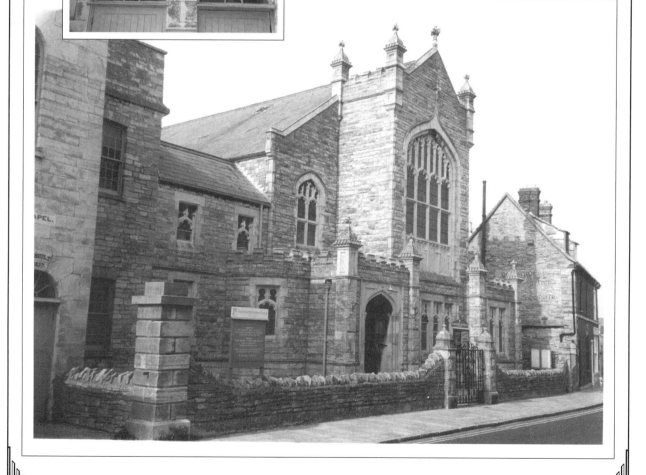

Above:
Memorial to Revd Thomas Oldfeld Bartlett, who obtained the additional burial ground in 1826, photographed by Colin Graham before it was demolished and partly rebuilt into the corner of the Parish Church.

Above:
John Mowlem's pyramid, erected in 1854 for wife Susannah in Guernsey granite from the contractor's own quarry, dominating the Victorian cemetery west of Northbrook Road.

The elegant organ as centre-piece in the Methodist Church, photographed by Rodney Legg in 1990.

*Gates of the 20th-century Swanage Cemetery, with photographer Colin Graham
having found a dog that could read, beside Washpond Lane at Godlingston.*

The modern Swanage Cemetery, with an architecturally plain little chapel, was established across seven acres of former Bankes Estate land beside Washpond Lane, Godlingston. It opened in 1931 and has since been expanded.

The brick-built Emmanuel Baptist Church on the south side of the High Street, beside the corner with Howard Road, had its foundation stones laid by covenanter Beatrice Ellen Beebe and Pastor James Wicks on 19 June 1920. Above, over the door, another tablet of Purbeck stone proclaims: 'To the glory of God this Chapel was erected and opened free of debt in answer to prayer. May 1921.'

All Saints Church, in Ulwell Road, stands on the corner with Redcliffe Road and is a suburban building of stone and pantiles of simple design with only a cross for embellishment. Built by George

Parsons of Swanage, in 1956–57, it cost £19 000. Its treasure, a gift from parishioners at Bingham's Melcombe, on the Dorset Downs, is an elegant classical font. Dated 1751, it has a circular bowl, with bay-leaf ornamentation and a wooden pineapple finial.

Other denominations include the Roman Catholic Church of the Holy Spirit and St Edward in Victoria Avenue, staffed by the Canons Regular of St John Lateran, and the Salvation Army in the Citadel in the High Street. The Plymouth Brethren meet in Victoria Avenue Chapel. King's Church gathers in the Vista Hall in the Municipal Caravan Park. The Religious Society of Friends, aka the Quakers, use the Rectory Classroom on Church Hill. Herston Methodist Church is in Bell Street. One of the huts of the German prisoner-of-war camp beside Darkie Lane became Ulwell Mission Hall.

Left: *The Anchor Inn on the north side of the eastern High Street, once the most prestigious establishment in the town, in the time of Elijah Vacher (standing proud), c.1880.*

Below: *Looking east along the south side of the High Street in 1896 from Boult's Saddlery to the White Swan (behind the cart) with the sign for the Anchor Hotel ('Inn' no longer) projecting from the left.*

The Ship Hotel, with landlord Bassum's name above the door, opposite Albion Place with the Round House on the corner (behind the carter) towards the eastern end of the High Street.

Ship Hotel (centre), advertising 'Strong's Noted Romsey Ales & Stout' seen from the west with Victorian ladies in the foreground and the White Swan Inn (behind) and the Round House (right).

Chapter 12

HOSTELRIES AND HOTELS

Looking eastwards down the upper section of the High Street from the Black Swan (right), in about 1888 when John Dowland was the publican, before replacement of the fencing by railings (with pastor Joseph Powell standing opposite).

Approaching from the west, the 18th-century Black Swan, in the High Street at Townsend, has the best inn sign in town, with twirls of wrought iron holding its bird. The quarrymen also held court in the former New Inn – aptly renamed the Stonemason, but since closed – opposite the Methodist Church on Spring Hill, and at the Red Lion and the Anchor. They met the fisher folk in the White Swan and around the corner in the Ship Inn and at the White Hart, now re-named the Purbeck Hotel. Others include the Globe and Royal Oak, and the Railway Inn of 1886 which narrowly failed to celebrate its centenary, closing in 1981 before proper reinstatement of the line.

One hostelry, in particular, made a successful transition from inn to hotel. The Anchor Hotel is an 18th-century bow-windowed hostelry with a long frontage on the north side of the High Street towards its seaward end, which was a place of style and pretensions long before the town became a popular resort. Its gig-and-fly was the only public transport in early-19th-century Swanage, though hardly a mass-transit vehicle, given that the hire of it and the two horses, plus driver in leather and a red-coat, would be at the then colossal price of £1.10s.0d. for a ride to Wareham.

The Anchor extended its elitist monopoly by providing the town's first bathing machine. This again was restricted by price to wealthy visitors and residents. One horse and a male attendant were required for its passage to the beach. A nurse then supervised its use to ensure that everything was proper and decent. Watering in early-19th-century Swanage cost the equivalent of a world cruise today.

Upstaging the Anchor would be the Swanage Hotel of William Morton Pitt, who bought the seafront Manor House and built Marine Villa as his summer house in 1825, spending the next two years turning it into the Swanage Hotel. This was his last major endeavour, at the age of 71, achieved by adding two wings and a stable block, parts of which survive at the heart of the present building. He lived to see Swanage Hotel elevated into the Royal Victoria Hotel following the visit of Princess Victoria and her mother, the Duchess of Kent, for the night of 7 August 1833. Swanage found its way on to the social map.

After Pitt's death, in 1836, it was sold at auction, being the second of his estate's 39 lots in a sale held in 1838, being described as the 'well-known celebrated hotel at Swanage' containing 'every convenience and accommodation which can be required'. There was:

... a lawn, fenced with iron rails, in the front, capital gardens and yards attached, and between the front of the hotel and the sea is a private pier or quay handsomely built and finished as a place for embarking and landing, whilst it forms a marine promenade for the visitors.

Having then had Victoria's son and heir, the future Edward VII, visiting as a 15-year-old on his walking tour of September 1856, the Royal Victoria Hotel continued to boast standards fit for the royalty, which were upheld in Queen Victoria's final decade by Miss Isabella Vincent. She continued to run a tight ship, for staff and visitors alike, until 1923. She would have turned in her grave as it ceased to be an hotel in 1972 after suffering the down-market spectacle of stallholders regularly infesting the elegant lawns. The next owner, Ray Beck, converted it to flats.

Around the corner, facing Peveril Downs from Seymer Road, Pitt built Belvedere House in 1828. It is a graceful Regency terrace in three-storey stucco with a slate roof, built originally as three houses, though now there are two, with the northern part being known as Belvedere Lodge. Seymer Road was named for Grace Seymer, Pitt's second wife.

For nearly a century the elegant four-storey lines of the Hotel Grosvenor graced the southern sweep of Swanage Bay. Its older, eastern wing incorporated The Grove, being the 'marine residence' built for the Coventry family on the site of an old quarry below Peveril Downs, in 1838. It became the home of retired London contractor Thomas Docwra in 1866. He enlarged it in 1892. Edwin Williams then built Sunnydown and Peveril Tower (renamed Rockleigh) in the grounds, between 1892 and 1895.

Further expansion on a grand scale, turning the core buildings into the Hotel Grosvenor, took place under the ownership of the Exton family who hired Nottingham architect Walter Hickson to build the central section in 1902 and add the west wing in 1905. This wing was given an extended frontage by George Hardy in 1927. The total length of frontage, facing seawards, was 400 feet.

The Exton Hotels Company Ltd boasted that the Grosvenor's dining room, seating 150 guests:

... both as regards comfort and position, is unrivalled by any hotel on the South Coast, having terrace windows extending over 80 feet, with most delightful views of the Swanage Bay and Purbeck Hills.

The brochure also lists the accommodation, including:

... a Spacious Lounge, fitted with Vita glass, attractive Sun Lounge, Dining, Smoking, Ballroom and Recreation Rooms, in addition to about 110 Bedrooms and Private Sitting Rooms.

It then goes on to describe the Annexe and the apartments:

The bedrooms, the majority of which overlook the sea, are comfortably furnished and are fitted with hot and cold running water, and gas fires. They are approached by accessible corridors and an electric lift. A few of the first floor bedrooms have French windows opening on to self-contained balconies, overlooking the bay.

King George VI and wartime Prime Minister Winston Churchill hosted dinner at the Grosvenor for a galaxy of top American, British and Canadian generals after the huge Exercise Smash practice landings for the invasion of Normandy, which were held to a realistic backdrop of bombs and live-fire on the look-alike beach of Studland Bay, on 18 April 1944.

Closure and demolition of Swanage's largest hotel came in 1985–86 and resulted from a controversial and abortive attempt by Durrant Developments to replace the Grosvenor with a yacht marina and yuppie seaside village. Some luxury continental-style villas were built in 1987 but receivership brought about the collapse of the more grandiose plans. The Hotel Grosvenor remains a fond memory, as Lieutenant-Colonel Archie Strange-Boston proved by sending me its souvenir brochure from Louisiana, and Swanage author Merle Chacksfield summed up as she looked towards an empty space from the Mowlem Restaurant:

I certainly miss its gracious lines which added to the tone of Swanage Bay. I shall always remember the evening sunlight shining on those elegant buildings bordering the deep turquoise of the sea and happy times I have spent there with my mother taking afternoon tea in its quiet, relaxed surroundings.

Merle Chacksfield and husband Bob would do their best to bring discerning visitors to the town by being pivotal in twinning Swanage with Rüdesheim. Two-way traffic to the attractive wine-producing town on the Rhine, in Germany, has been taking place since 1985.

The physical loss of the Grosvenor and the conversion of the Royal Victoria to flats reduced Swanage's three purpose-built 19th-century hotels to a single upstart, the Grand Hotel of 1898 which with the Monte Rosa began the process of turning the fields of north Swanage into New Swanage suburb. Taking their place, however, is Purbeck House Hotel in George Burt's splendid house, preserving the town's best domestic building in a style that becomes it.

The Royal Victoria Hotel, as it looked out across to boats on the slipway, photographed in the 1970s.

The immense frontage of the Hotel Grosvenor was the dominating landmark beside Swanage Bay.

The size and extent of the Hotel Grosvenor seen from the air, being photographed from the north-east.

The Hotel Grosvenor, painted in its heyday in the 1930s, from the old pier.

Above: *Flag-decked street, for King George V's golden jubilee in 1935, showing Institute Road with Stead and Simpson boot-makers (left) and Barclays Bank (opposite).*

Below: *Procession along Institute Road in celebration of the King George V's golden jubilee in 1935, with the Westminster Bank being the prominent building behind the Union Flag.*

Chapter 13
POLICE AND PUBLIC

The Blind House, a lock-up behind the Town Hall, was an archetypal 'slammer' or 'cooler'. Like so much of old Swanage it has a wordy and worthy inscription: 'Erected For the Prevention of Vice & Immorality by the Friends of Religion and good Order A.D. 1803.' This tiny cell, the local prison, originally stood 'on ye north side of ye Church Tower' and was then moved into the south-west corner of the churchyard when the church was rebuilt in 1859. Boys from the quarries would stand above it, at the top of some steps, and bombard the door with stones when a drunk was locked inside.

Great events tended to find Swanage. It was on the front-line for seafaring disasters and the comings and goings of warfare. Princess Victoria's visit in 1833 had been a direct consequence of convenient geography, for a trip over the water to Cowes, rather than a direct interest in the town.

Likewise the excitement of 1869 when William Trask, the son of a Yeovil blacksmith, decided upon the seaside at Swanage as his objective when he set out to ride his newly-made penny-farthing across the widest

The Blind House, a lock-up behind the Town Hall, provided in 1803.

available cross-section of the Dorset countryside. He estimated the distance as 48 miles and would be the first person, so far as is recorded, to arrive in Swanage by bicycle. This innovative form of transport caused considerable excitement among spectators of all ages. The new-fashioned 'horse' fascinated the fishermen and quarry workers who wondered how it could be mounted and manoeuvred: 'Inhabitants have had few opportunities of studying the breed before and are greatly puzzled how the queer-looking apparatus is kept upright.'

Before this new age of mechanical mobility there was little need for law enforcement apart from during instances of public disorder. The first Swanage policeman was John Cripps, provided by Judge David Jardine, who had adopted the town in the 1850s. Cripps had a close shave at the hands of the natives in a Christmas Eve riot in 1851. 'There was a mob of boys and men to the number of one hundred,' John Mowlem wrote in his diary, continuing:

... had it not been for Mrs Melmoth I think the poor fellow must have lost his life. I was half a day yesterday at the Rectory with Dr Wilcox and Mr Serrell taking the depositions of sundry persons respecting the attack. I sincerely hope the guilty will be brought to justice and transported if possible. William Croft is the ring-leader of the party and a worse man there cannot be; he is a bad husband and a drunkard to boot.

Several duly appeared before Wareham magistrates on 30 December but Mowlem would be disappointed by the result and despaired: 'The magistrates don't know their duty. I look at them as a set of old ladies. A fine for the rabble here is of no use.' The general level of this penalty was £2.10s.0d., doubling to £5 for William Croft.

A favourite Swanage expletive, to which Croft would have responded, was 'tatty greens'. It would be used by William Saunders who, with a group of 30 men outside the Ship Hotel in 1875, kept shouting and repeating the words at gentleman Charles Robinson. The latter responded with his stick, hitting Saunders, and would be fined £1. The cause of the ill-feeling seems to have been land that the Robinson family had bought, with the result that quarrymen had been issued with notices to quit.

Another 'quarry dispute' took place opposite the memorial to Albert the Good, at the top of Court Hill, when men 'in fighting mood' kept shouting 'tatty greens' at Mr and Mrs William Trayte of Herston House. That was followed by a fight in the Black Swan and fines of 10 shillings plus 6s.8d. costs were imposed on each of the two convicted assailants. 'We want to hear no more of the quarry disputes,' the magistrate said.

Swanage had a reputation as a rough place. Poole people used the epithet 'Turks' for its inhabitants, who visited the port on the market boat, and regarded them as 'vulgar in their manner and displaying general ignorance of commercial and business conventions'. Sir Charles Robinson made it clear that he regarded George Burt as a 'Turk', by describing him as a vulgar upstart, and snubbing 'the King' by refusing to drink the water he had piped into town, instead constructing his own reservoir to supply Newton Manor. Those from Swanage who moved to Wareham were dubbed 'Turkeys'. Both terms had far stronger connotations than would be apparent today, for the Turks had been notorious for cutting off their prisoners' testicles. Some British ex-soldiers travelled the countryside to reveal their mutilations and receive handouts from public funds.

The Police Station in Argyle Road, like much else in Victorian Swanage, was the creation of shrewd developer George Burt. Plans for its building were discussed at the Dorset Midsummer Sessions in Shire Hall, Dorchester, during June 1881. Burt had offered to build the station with cells and living quarters for two officers. The cost would be £600 and Burt proposed paying this, and then leasing the completed building to the county for 15 years, at an annual rent of £24.

Captain Amyatt E. Amyatt, the Chief Constable, said he understood Mr Burt intended erecting a Town Hall, a short distance away in the High Street, and that this would be available for magisterial purposes. Lord Eldon pointed out that all this was news to the divisional magistrates. His reported comments were:

The present arrangement by which prisoners had to be removed from Swanage to Wareham for trial was doubtlessly inconvenient but he understood Mr Burt was going to construct a railway and then it would be less inconvenient. (Laughter.) He was not sure the erection of this police station would be a gain. At present no petty sessions were held there, and anybody wanting to get a summons had to go to Wareham. He should like this question postponed until the next sessions in order more definite plans might be proposed.

Delay was not an option, T.B. Hanham responded, saying he had known Swanage for the previous 15 years, 'during which time it [had] completely changed'. The suggested site was central and 'there [would] be difficulty in delaying the matter'. He described Swanage as a place 'considerably increasing in value' and added that it was 'very doubtful if the county [would] receive this offer again at the same price'.

As in the matter of the railway, despite the joke, manipulative entrepreneur George Burt had once again scored a victory over the reticent Purbeck aristocracy. Burt's own mansion, Purbeck House, had its deterrent for potential miscreants characteristically etched in stone beside the driveway: 'BEWARE OF DOG. CHAINED DAY. LOOSE NIGHT.' Allegedly there was no dog – but that's the art of crime prevention.

George Burt's warning to potential miscreants, built into the entrance of Purbeck House.

Chapter 14
PEOPLE AND PERSONALITIES

Gypsy knife-grinders, passing the newly-built Arcade in the High Street, which was designed by George Crickmay in 1888, as seven shops for stone merchant Nathan Chinchen White.

Starting as I mean to continue, with personages in alphabetical order, the de facto ruler of Penang was **Lieutenant-Colonel Sir Arthur (Robert) Adams (1861–1937)** who retired from Malaya to Rockleigh on Peveril Point. He had only been in the position of exercising short-term direct rule over the colony's Eastern Archipelago, during 1910–11, but frequently found himself with wider and longer powers of one-man governance as Solicitor-General of Penang and Commandant of the Penang Volunteers, from 1899 to 1919.

Wildlife artist **Roy Aplin** was born in Swanage and began painting at an early age. In 1980, during illness, he was encouraged by artist Eric Peake to concentrate on painting and began specialising in watercolour with added gouache. He was talent spotted at the National Cage and Aviary Show in 1995 and commissioned as a result to paint 'the perfect specimen for breeding and judging standards'. Commercially, he finds that paintings of owls and other raptors sell worldwide, though he still keeps his hand in as a Wareham carpenter.

Churchman **Revd Thomas Oldfeld Bartlett (1786–1841)** was the rector of Swanage and Worth Matravers for 21 years and was instrumental in acquiring the new cemetery on the slope opposite the south-east corner of St Mary's Parish Church in 1826. His memorial stone records that he 'was by his own desire interred within this burial ground, obtained through his exertions', but it is now displaced, having been moved to the north-east corner of the actual church.

Aircraft designer and inventor **Leslie Everett Jeffrey 'Baron' Baynes (1902–89)** is buried in Swanage Cemetery, Godlingston, beneath a Purbeck marble gravestone with a finely sculpted head and relief of his Baynes Bee creation. He built novel little flying machines such as an auxiliary sail-plane with a Carden engine which, together with its propeller, could be retracted into the fuselage. It was displayed to the Royal Aeronautical Society meeting at Heathrow, which was then Fairey Aviation's aerodrome, on 5 May 1935. Baynes was pioneering ultra-lights, such as the two-seater, twin-engined Baynes Bee. Only 29 feet 10 inches in length, it was put into construction at Heston, by Carden-Baynes Aircraft Limited. Powered by two 40-horsepower Carden engines, it was taken up by Hubert Broad for its maiden flight, in April 1937. It and similar frivolities were out of step with the spirit of the times and would be squeezed from the sky by the gathering clouds of European war. During the conflict Baynes devised the conversion of the American-built Boston bomber into a Havoc night-fighter that carried the Turbinlite airborne searchlight. Bitterness marred his post-war years. Baynes was positive that his ideas had been stolen, by the Americans and others, and blamed the Ministry of Supply for blocking a paper he was to have presented to the Royal Aeronautical Society in 1949. They called in his plans for a 1000-mph variable-wing fighter and classified them top secret. For fun he devised his sail-plane with a retractable propeller and engine, which could turn itself into a glider, but he felt it should have been his destiny to make the British equivalent of the F-111. He regarded it as a waste of national talent that he was running an antique shop in Corfe Castle.

Irascible **Dr Andrew Bell (1753–1832)** was Swanage's eccentric and often absentee rector from 1801 to 1809. He had worked for the East India Company but ill-health forced his return to England, with a £25 000 fortune and a substantial pension. The Swanage living was little more than a formal position though Bell did effective social work and introduced the women of the town to the trade of flax spinning and making straw-plaited bonnets. Bell's time in Swanage was marred by his unfortunate marriage, in 1800, to Agnes Barclay. This was depicted as persecution by De Quincey in his *Essay on Coleridge*. 'Perhaps the most marked feature in Bell's character was this love of money,' says his unflattering entry in *The Dictionary of National Biography*. His other interest was education and in this he was a strident self-publicist. In India, in 1789, he pioneered the mutual instruction method of teaching, in which the brightest eight-year-olds taught the infants. This became known as 'The Madras System'. Bell's writing, on this chosen subject, began with *An Experiment in Education* in 1797, and expanded into English social issues with *A Sermon on the Education of the Poor* in 1807. *A Sermon on the Education of the Poor in the Principles of our Holy Religion and in Habits of Useful Industry* was published the following year and eventually led to the creation of National Schools as the educational wing of the Anglican Church. In Swanage, Bell Street was named for him, south from Herston Cross.

Escaped train robber **Ronnie Biggs (born 1929)** lived at Swanage in 1960, three years before a Royal Mail train, the Glasgow to London express, was stopped at Sears Crossing, Linslade, Buckinghamshire, at 03.00 hours on 8 August 1963. All told 16 other villains were involved in the heist which netted £2 631 684. Biggs served his criminal apprenticeship in Dorset: 'I did a lot of burglaries and thefts and appeared at Dorchester Quarter Sessions, where I got 18 months.' Having been convicted of the train robbery he would break out of Wandsworth Prison in 1965 and spend his life in Rio de Janeiro, until returning to England and custody in May 2001.

The composer **Sir Arthur Bliss (1891–1975)**, Master of the Queen's Musick from 1953, was patron of the Purbeck Festival of Music. He regularly attended concerts at St Mary's Church, Swanage, and Lady St Mary's Church, Wareham. His widow, Lady Bliss, continued to attend these events.

Children's author **Enid Blyton (1897–1968)**, the best-selling English writer of the 20th century, 'always spent her holidays at Swanage'. She spotted ex-Guardsman Christopher Rone (1915–90), an archetypal village bobby, on his bicycle in the lanes around Studland. Rone was immortalised as PC Plod in the Noddy stories. He retired to Carey Close, Wareham, and dined out on his claim to fame. Enid Blyton and her husband, Harley Street surgeon Kenneth Darrell-Waters, bought the Isle of Purbeck Golf Club in 1951. They ran it until 1965, on Bankes Estate land – now National Trust owned – on the Studland side of the Ulwell Gap. Miss Blyton became a familiar summertime adjunct to the landscape as she worked on her books on a table outside the original clubhouse. This stood on the west side of the Swanage to Studland road at Dean Hill, a short distance beyond the fork leading uphill towards Corfe Castle, and was affectionately known as the 'Little Tin Hut'. She typed directly on to the page. 'I think straight on to my typewriter,' she remarked. 'It's the best way of writing vividly.' Her prodigious output totalled some 700 titles. All were full of exclamation marks and celebrated the simple joys of childhood. Enid Blyton took an active part in Swanage life and was for many years the president of the Swanage Regatta and Carnival Organisation. She would stay with her daughters at the Hotel Grosvenor and became something of a cultural institution.

One of Nelson's captains, **Admiral Sir Charles Bullen (1769–1853)** lived at Newton Cottage, which is now known as Heather Close. He commanded the 100-gun HMS *Britannia* as the fourth ship in the weather line that was led by HMS *Victory* in Lord Nelson's Division at the Battle of Trafalgar on 21 October 1805. He was then Captain Bullen and would have a long post-war career, being knighted in 1835 and advanced to the rank of Admiral, in 1852.

George Burt, stone merchant by trade and the town's top mason in more ways than one, seen here in full regalia.

Victorian entrepreneur and developer **George Burt (1816–94)** was described as 'the King of Swanage' by the novelist Thomas Hardy, who observed that he was rougher in speech than would be expected after his years in London, 'being the ordinary type of Dorsetman, self-made by trade, whenever one of the county does self-make himself, which is not often'. Burt was the nephew and business associate of wealthy contractor John Mowlem. Succeeding him as boss of the Swanage stone trade, Burt edged its operations out of the town and began to transform the old stone port into a seaside spa, starting the first steamer service. Having rebuilt Purbeck House in the High Street, in 1875, incorporating numerous pieces of old London, he went on to embellish the town generally and the surrounding countryside, and sold building plots on his Durlston Park Estate.

Heir apparent **Sir John Mowlem Burt (1845–1918)**, son of George Burt and great nephew of John Mowlem, propelled the contracting dynasty of John Mowlem & Co. Ltd into royal commissions. He was knighted for his refurbishment of Westminster Abbey for the coronation of Edward VII in 1902.

Stone merchant **Robert Burt (1788–1847)**, the father of George Burt, lived at No. 1 Victoria Terrace, Swanage, and has an elaborate fluted column above his grave in the old parish churchyard, on the slope south east of St Mary's Church. In 1812 he married Laetitia ('Lettie') Manwell (1786–1851) and their children were George (b.1816), Elizabeth (b.1818), Robert (b.1821), Charles (b.1823), Francis (b.1825) and Susannah (b.1829).

Retired Christchurch headmistress **Merle Chacksfield**, who pioneered music and language studies with young children and published educational books, retired with husband Bob to Rocquiane Court in Ilminster Road. She has produced a series of West Country studies on gutsy aspects of the past millennium, starting with *Smuggling Days* and *The Dorset and Somerset Rebellion* and moving on to the *Armada 1585* and *Glorious Revolution 1688*. Closer to home, on the other side of Godlingston Hill, she researched the history of the Isle of Purbeck Golf Club for its centenary in 1992. Appreciating other pleasures in life, the Chacksfields were instrumental in selecting the German wine-town of Rüdesheim am Rhein for twinning with Swanage, in 1986.

London solicitor **Sir Geoffrey Abdy Collins (1888–1982)** was a member of the council of the Law Society (1931–56) and knighted during his term as its president (1951–52). He lived at Mullion, on the Ballard Estate, on the Studland side of the hill.

Colonial soldier **Captain Frederick Coventry (1820–46)** of The Grove, Swanage, and the 29th Regiment, has a memorial in St Mary's Church. It records that 'this most amiable and promising young officer' was spared in the Battle of Sobraon, against the Sikhs on 10 February 1846, 'but he fell victim to the climate of India' and died on 29 July, being buried at Kussowlie.

The medical family of **Delamotte** has its memorials on the wall of St Mary's Church, including Henry Digby Cotes Delamotte (1796–1874) 'for over fifty years a surgeon of this town' and George Cotes Delamotte (1829–1922) of Osborne House, 'who for many years was a medical practitioner of this town and was churchwarden of this parish for 17 years'.

Naval hero **Joseph Edmonds (1720–94)** retired to Swanage. His monument, above the vestry door in St

Mary's Church, shows two ships engaged in battle:

Commander of the Defiance *of 24 guns whose bravery in conquering a French ship of superior force in 1758 was generously rewarded by the underwriters and merchants of the City of London.*

He died at Swanage on 26 September 1794 at the age of 74, perhaps when news reached England of the death of his eldest son, James, in Jamaica on 5 July 1794. James, aged 33, was in command of the *New Albion*. The year of tragedy was to continue for Joseph's widow, Priscilla, with the death of their youngest son, 29-year-old John, commander of the *Dorset* 'who was kill'd gallantly defending his ship against the French off the island of Cuba, 21st October 1794'. Priscilla Edmonds survived them and died on 18 March 1821, at the age of 75.

A non-person, as far as Swanage is concerned, was Antarctic adventurer **Petty Officer Edgar 'Taffy' Evans** who was given a plaque on a stone terraced house at 82 High Street, Swanage. It transpired, however, that its occupant had been a different Edgar Evans, rather than the one who joined *Discovery* in 1910 for Captain Robert Falcon Scott's expedition to the South Pole. That Taffy was one of the five to make 'the final assault on the Pole, which was reached on 18 January 1912', and during which expedition 'all five men died on the 820-mile return journey across the ice'. The High Street plaque, which belongs in Swansea rather than Swanage – the same number of letters – went on to give the memorable quotation from the annals of heroism: 'To strive, to seek, to find, and not to yield.' Scott and his four gallant comrades perished in March 1912. They had been beaten to the target by Roald Amundsen, his four Norwegian companions, and their 17 huskies, who arrived at the South Pole on 14 December 1911. Scott had chosen not to take dogs and the five Britons each pulled a sledge weighing 190 pounds but containing inadequate rations. They starved to death in a blizzard in the attempt at returning to their base.

Sometime Leader of the Labour Party **Michael Foot MP (born 1913)** went to Forres School in Swanage before moving on to Leighton Park School, Oxford, and Wadham College, Oxford.

Museum director **Sir Richard Foster (1941–2001)**, who ran the National Museums and Galleries on Merseyside, was found dead in Swanage Bay on the morning of 8 March 2001. Portland Coastguard said there were no suspicious circumstances and the police confirmed that death was believed to have been due to drowning. Chris Smith, the Culture Secretary, expressed shock and sadness and paid tribute to Sir Richard, who left a wife and three children.

Painting within a stone's throw of the seaside in central Swanage, with a view across to Ballard Down, surrealist painter **Brian Graham** produces Turneresque landscapes and seascapes. His 'Tempest', for example, features the eye of a storm. From a first exhibition in Poole Arts Centre in 1979 he has progressed to Bettles Gallery, Ringwood, and the Hart Gallery in London. He enthused to Vivienne Light about the sense of past and place that Swanage offers:

Nothing else can really get near it. If I had to do figurative studies or still life it would mean nothing to me. Here I'm in the studio which looks out over the hillside. The sea is over there, which you can see very clearly, barrows up on the hills there – that ancient set called Nine Barrow Down you can just about catch sight of on the western edge there – and you can see the clouds going across the bay there. It's beautiful.

Radio comedian **Tony Hancock (1924–68)** went to school in Swanage. He boarded at Durlston Court School. His family had moved to Bournemouth from Birmingham in 1927. With the onset of puberty he became introverted but he found relief from depression after taking up acting during the war when he joined the RAF Gang Show. Radio fame came as tutor in *Educating Archie* from 1951 to 1953 which resulted in his own show, *Hancock's Half Hour*, running from 1954 to 1963 and transferring to television in 1956. His film roles included *The Rebel* in 1961 and *The Punch and Judy Man* in 1963. Psychological problems from childhood were never properly overcome. As a chain-smoking perfectionist he became dubbed 'The Anxiety Man' by the newspapers and he always found it difficult to incorporate women into his act. He would kill himself in Sydney in 1968.

Wessex author **Thomas Hardy (1840–1928)**, though not directly related to the Hardy family of Swanage, lived in the town through the autumn and winter of 1875–76. With first wife Emma he took lodgings in West End Cottage, in the cul-de-sac off Seymer Road to the west of Peveril Downs open space. It was the home of 'an invalid captain of smacks and ketches' and the period introduced Thomas to the realities and risks of life at sea. He was told of the occasional naked bodies that were washed inshore. 'The sea undresses them,' was how ships' masters put it, as they explained that the victims of drowning and shipwreck floated in with the tide from Portland and the west. 'He has read well who has learnt that there is more to read outside books than inside them,' Hardy wrote in his diary. During the winter he completed *The Hand of Ethelberta: A Comedy in Chapters*. This light-hearted novel tackles the Victorian obsession with class, as a contemporary satire, set in Bournemouth and Purbeck. Swanage appears as Knollsea, with the 'little steamer *Speedwell*' setting off from the 1859-built pier to Cherbourg, where Ethelberta visits her aunt. Hardy probably already knew Swanage, having been involved in the design of St Mark's Church at

West End Cottage, off Seymer Road, was home for author Thomas Hardy and first wife Emma.

Herston during his short working life as an architect. He returned to the town on 31 October 1919 to join the Bishop of Salisbury in the opening of Swanage Children's Hospital at Hill Side in Peveril Road.

Construction engineer **William Masters Hardy**, from the Swanage branch of the family, undertook his biggest project in Kent where he built a sea wall in 1871, extending '1700 feet long and 22 feet high, at the bottom of the chalk cliff on the west side of Ramsgate Harbour'. Closer to home, he restored Studland's pre-Conquest Parish Church, in 1881, though with much more tolerance for its antiquities than would have been shown by the average Victorian builder. In retirement he filled his time with writing, becoming the first Swanage historian and leaving a wealth of memories and contemporary anecdotes, which lost nothing in the telling as he wove them into a series of delightful and compelling reminiscences.

The body of newly-wed **Mrs Jean Mary Iliffe (1927–73)** was discovered by Police Constable Peter Redfern, beneath the food in the freezer in the passageway of her home at No. 2 Grosvenor Road, Swanage. Her dog was howling beside it. Painter and decorator Alan Scott and PC P. Harrison had entered the house after Mrs Iliffe failed to make her customary telephone call to her mother. First they found her semi-conscious husband. Terence Iliffe, who was born in 1921, would be revived in a London hospital after having haemorrhaged from a drugs overdose. There were no less than eight suicide notes in Mr Iliffe's clear handwriting. Rumours spread

around Swanage that Mrs Iliffe had been stabbed but it was established by Winchester pathologist Peter Pullar on 5 December 1973 that she had died from strangulation. Her body was still warm when she was put into the freezer with the result that meat piled on top of her defrosted with the body heat. Terence Iliffe would stand trial for murder at Winchester Crown Court in 1974. Balding, with long grey sideburns, he was immaculate in his suit, and looked and spoke like an old-fashioned bank manager. He denied murder but would be convicted on a majority verdict of 10-2. The court heard that the former twice-widowed Mrs Jean King still had a soft-spot for an ex-boyfriend. For engineer Terence Iliffe it was his fourth marriage. Just 18 days after their wedding Jean played 'Spanish Eyes' on the record deck. It was her old favourite; their song for Jean and former partner Joe Grygiel. She proceeded to phone him in America. 'I love you,' she said. 'I have always loved you.' Then events in the Grosvenor Road household, which had been Mrs Iliffe's home for a number of years, deteriorated into a fracas and worse on 3 December 1973. Mr Iliffe punched and strangled her, it would be alleged, though he denied premeditation. Sentencing him to life imprisonment, Mr Justice Wien said he would have passed the same sentence even if the jury had cleared him of murder, and found him guilty of manslaughter instead.

Brilliant law writer **David Jardine (1794–1860)** adopted Swanage whilst it was still a quarrying town. The Recorder for Bath, who came from Weybridge, was 'very learned and ingenious' to quote Macaulay, who used Jardine's work as a source for his own popularisations of English history. *A Reading on the use of Torture in the Criminal Law of England previously to the Commonwealth* appeared in 1837 and was followed by a study of the *Gunpowder Plot* and *Remarks on the Law and Expediency of requiring the presence of Accused Persons at Coroners' Inquisitions*, which appeared in 1846. In and around Swanage he has his memorials, ranging from the clock in St Mary's Church (he paid half its £240 cost, in 1859) to the Judge's Seats (inscribed 'D.J. 1852: Rest and be Thankful') on Peveril Downs and Ballard Down.

Welsh impressionist painter **Augustus John (1878–1961)** began his multiple associations with Dorset in 1899 when he stayed in Swanage, at Mrs Katherine Everett's boarding house, Peveril Tower. He returned the following year to seduce Viennese aristocrat Maria Katerina. 'The country here is lovely beyond words,' he wrote. 'Corfe Castle and neighbourhood would make you mad with painter's cupidity.' John returned to Peveril Tower for his honeymoon with Ida Nettleship in 1900. She would die of peritonitis in 1907 and he moved to Alderney Manor, Poole, and a debauched bohemian lifestyle that would make him a living legend. He never lost his love of the Purbeck landscape and took every opportunity to return to the Square and Compass at Worth Matravers.

The doyen of cricket commentators, **Brian Johnston (1912–94)** lived in Burlington Road, Swanage, having moved there from Acton, at Langton Matravers, in 1967. Before that he was at Cerne Abbas. 'Johnners', as the Old Etonian was known throughout the sporting and broadcasting world, also compered the *Down Your Way* radio programmes and recorded a total of 733 between 1972 and 1987. Sportingly, he concluded his innings at that point, because to have continued would have exceeded the achievement of his predecessor, Franklin Engelmann. He is commemorated by a plaque in Durlston Country Park. 'Brian always came up here in all weathers, with the children and the dogs – whether they liked it or didn't,' said his widow, Pauline Johnston. 'The wetter and colder it was the more we loved it.'

Swanage became a murder scene with the finding of the body of **Diana Kemp (1949–69)** in a ditch at the Ulwell Gap, a few yards from a bus stop below the western end of Ballard Down. She was found on 30 November 1969, wearing the remains of a blue mini-dress, but her underwear and stockings were missing. Diana had left her home in Elizabeth Avenue, Christchurch, at 20.15 hours on Thursday 16 October 1969. Her parents assumed she had gone out with her boyfriend, Robert, whom she had telephoned earlier in the evening, but that had been to make arrangements for the following night. She never returned home. Her shoulder bag was found at 20.35 hours on the Thursday, lying on the main road at Rushford Warren, Mudeford, and taken to her parents. Diana worked as a secretary for estate agents Goadsby and Harding and was described by her mother as 'the centre of attention' at parties. She suffered with glandular fever and it was hoped that she might have lost her memory. Her father feared that there must be more to it than that: 'After all, a handbag is a girl's most treasured possession.' She was known to have a dangerous predilection for hitch-hiking but there was no suspect driver nor any reported sightings.

The negative single clue, when her body was found, would be the absence of Diana's watch. This was then traced to Ashley Road Furniture Centre in Parkstone. Not only did dealer David Taylor have the Pontiac-brand lady's wrist watch but he recalled full details of how it came into his possession on 26 November 1969. He had bought it from a 25-year-old, giving him a £1 note, and recalled the man's conversation. This included a casual reference to a tape recorder in the window. The seller of the watch said this was 'just like a mate's machine'. Police regarded this as 'a long-shot' but everything started

to fall into place. Mr Taylor had a record of the name and address of the 19-year-old seller of the tape recorder. The young man had a 25-year-old friend with whom he had been working as a cinema projectionist at the Regent in Christchurch. There was now a prime suspect, who had just departed from lodgings in Westbourne in a white Hillman, though he conveniently left a forwarding address. As a result, Ian George Troup would be arrested in Dulwich on 8 December 1969, and newspapers carrying news of the discovery of Diana's body were found in his car. Troup admitted selling the watch but said he had found it in Boscombe Gardens. He turned out to be something of a loner, who liked Swanage – saying he had lived there – and spent most of his time model-making ships from plastic kits. Standing trial at Winchester, he pleaded not guilty to murder but admitted giving Diana a lift and struggling with her after she had declined to have sex with him at Mudeford. He then drove to Swanage, to dump the body, when he realised she was dead. The jury convicted him of murder, on 12 March 1970, and he was sentenced to life imprisonment.

As one of history's asides, closing an era if not an enigma, **Dr M.R. 'Bob' Lawrence** died in Swanage in 1971. He was the elder brother of Lawrence of Arabia.

Archetypal aspects of seaside life were captured in raunchy postcards by **Donald McGill (1875–1962)** whose commemorative seat is in the High Street, beside the Library. 'King of the saucy postcard,' the inscription reads. Hundreds were painted and millions posted.

The artist **Padraig Macmiadhachain (born 1929)**, from Northern Ireland, has been painting in his cottage studio in central Swanage for nearly half a century. His basic technique is to knife-work thick oils in minimalist subjects suggested by boats, cliffs and the sea. Colours are inspired by the natural landscape. Purbeck stone, quarried yellow, soon weathers to grey. Coastal contrasts range from tar-painted cottages on Peveril Point through to the gleaming white of the Lighthouse around the corner on Anvil Point. He exhibits in London at the New Academy Gallery.

Surrealist painter **Paul Nash (1889–1946)** lived in Swanage in the 1930s. In 1935 he compiled the Dorset volume in the *Shell Guide* series, which broke new ground as he realised at the time. Acknowledging the influence of John Betjeman's predecessor for Cornwall, Nash wrote, 'I have, in the main, examined and admired the way he has treated each section, and then done something as different as possible'. The idiosyncratic result received lasting acclaim as the best guide book ever produced.

It ends with a list of instructions to the reader:

When you go to an inn ask for English food. If you are given badly cooked so-called French food kick up a row. Use your influence, short of committing sacrilege, to clear the simple and often beautiful interiors of country churches free from the cheap colour reproduction of sixth-rate religious paintings and other undignified rubbish occasionally to be found there. Use your influence by writing or speaking against the frequent attempts on the part of jerry-builders and those bodies which attempt to absorb whole tracts of the countryside from their more or less destructive activities. Protest, if you live in a town, against all unnecessary spoliation of period buildings. Give your support to any or all of the societies mentioned in the dedication.

There he named the Council for the Preservation of Rural England and the Society for the Protection of Ancient Buildings, as those 'to whom we owe what is left of England'.

Reluctant philosopher **Thomas Manwell (1751–1822)** opted out of the greatness that might have been, according to his memorial inscription which was written by Swanage rector Dr Andrew Bell. This recorded that 'unassisted by education' he had used 'the strength of a superior genius, and Nature for his guide' to break through 'the barrier to literature'. His 'degree of knowledge' was such that it 'might have ranked him with the first philosophers of the age'. Then comes Bell's 'but', explaining Manwell's flight from fame:

Being a child of solitude, his retired Meditations were far dearer to him than the acquirement of Fame; and if Charity, Humility, and Meekness, with Faith in a Redeemer, be Christianity, he was a perfect Christian.

Thomas Manwell died on 4 February 1822, leaving behind sundials rather than words, one of them having been placed on St Mary's Church. He must have made some impact upon his times in that the lane where he lived has since carried his name, being Manwell's Lane on the south side of the High Street, west of the Black Swan. Adjoining it now are Manwell Road and Manwell Drive.

Conservative politician **David Mellor (born 1949)**, the son of Wareham mathematics teacher Douglas H. Mellor, would become the best known old boy of the former Swanage Grammar School. Remembered in the town as a 'precious little swot', he left to study law at Cambridge, and was called to the bar in 1972. He was chosen, in preference to his close friend and contemporary John Major, to fight the labour-held seat of Putney in 1974. Five years later he was in the House of Commons, and became the first of that intake to climb the ministerial ladder, in 1981. 'One of the most promising political careers in modern times,' saw him rise to become Minister for the Arts and then Secretary of State for the Heritage, in April 1992, which encompassed sport as well as culture and led to the tabloid press dubbing him the 'Fun Minister'. Ivan Fallon would chart his final two months in office in the *Sunday Times* of 27 September 1992:

In many ways he was the classic case of hubris, an excess of ambition and pride which would inevitably lead to ruin. There is nothing lean and hungry about him – indeed, his podginess is the true reflection of a practised sybarite. He struck his critics forcibly as overly ambitious, self-satisfied and cocky, the type of man that needed to be taken down a peg or two.

The first peg would be in the shapely form of Antonia de Sancha. It led to headlines about the minister and the actress and culminated with the *Sun* classic of 'Toe job to no job'. He quit at last after 'the double whammy' of guilt by association, that an innocent enough fortnight in Marbella was at the invitation of the daughter of the finance chief of the Palestinian Liberation Organisation, and happened to coincide with the Gulf War. In his resignation speech to Parliament, David Mellor said he was leaving the 'warmth of government for the icy wastes of the back benches', and ended with a reference to another ill-fated Putney man, Titus Oates of the Antarctic. Famous last words would be recalled: 'I am going out and it may be some time before I return.'

Quarrier and builder **John Mowlem (1788–1868)**, founder of the major contracting company that still carries his name, was born in a cottage at Carrant's Court, on the north side of Court Hill, Swanage. It was demolished in Edwardian times. Mowlem is buried in the Northbrook Road Cemetery, beneath a 20-foot pyramid of his own Guernsey granite. The maker's marks are for H. Bisson at Vale, in Guernsey. Mowlem's chance in life was given to him by fashionable London mason Henry Westmacott in a workshop at King's Row, Pimlico, in 1807. Mowlem became his foreman in 1816 but later walked out of the business, to start his own, by 1823. Soon he was leasing a wharf at Pimlico Basin, which is now beneath the forecourt of Victoria Station, and began paving much of the City of London. Relaying Blackfriars Bridge with Guernsey granite sets caused him so many difficulties that he took a boat to the Channel Islands and bought what became his own quarry, being a one-acre hillside field 'all of good blue granite'. Five stone dressers were employed and the granite was being shipped from Guernsey to London by 1840. There would be more astute land deals in Guernsey and his own brig, the *John Mowlem*, which conveyed stone to the capital. 'The great

John Mowlem, painted by Ramsay Richard Reinagle, in 1823.

Patrician bust of contractor John Mowlem, sculpted for his Mowlem Institute, which he gave to the town in 1865.

metropolis of the world,' Mowlem called it. Islanders virtually gave away their island with which he made a fortune. One quarry cost him £50 for its freehold and he would extract half-a-million tons from it. That was a tenth of a farthing per ton. In middle age, he took an increasing interest in Swanage, in anticipation of retirement. Victoria Terrace, facing the sea, had been built in 1835–36 and was owned by Robert Burt. Mowlem bought No. 2, a three-storey lodging house, in 1845. He built and moved into the castellated Herston House, a mile inland at Herston, in 1859, and played a leading part in the construction of Swanage's first timber-built pier. In 1860 he bought the pasture-lands northwards from The Brook to Bankes Estate land at Ulwell and Ballard Down. Mowlem then set about erecting commemorative monuments to the supposed naval battle between King Alfred and the Danes and Queen Victoria's Prince Consort, 'Albert the Good'. The Mowlem Institute followed, standing from 1863 to 1966, when it was rebuilt as the Mowlem, being expanded into a theatre and licensed restaurant. It was created 'for the benefit and mutual improvement of the working classes' and acted as a general meeting place and cultural centre at the heart of the seafront. Mowlem took on various civic duties in Swanage and filled his time as a magistrate and by using a highly diluted proportion of his talents to drain, level, pave and kerb the High Street and other roads. One was de Moulham Road, commemorating his family's centuries-old links with Swanage, on land he had bought parallel to Northbrook Road. He was a perfectionist of the trivial, fussing day-long in Swanage, to the irritation of those having to lay kerb stones. It was as the town's benefactor that he died in the 'old' Purbeck House in the High Street, in 1868, in the home of his wealthy nephew George Burt. That was before John Mowlem and Company Limited, now plc, started to prosper on the grand scale under Burt's management, beginning with the new Billingsgate Market in 1874, and winning royal commissions such as the major refurbishment of Westminster Abbey for Edward VII's coronation in 1902. The name remained synonymous with major construction work throughout the 20th century, from the Dorchester bypass to the new London Bridge, and Docklands Light Railway. Mowlem's former home, Herston House, would be demolished in 1967. He has been claimed as the model for John Galsworthy's 'Superior Dosset Forsyte' in his famous *Saga* and nephew George Burt as the model for 'Old Jolyon'.

The agriculturist **Edward Agar Horatio Nelson, 5th Earl Nelson (1886–1951)** managed landed estates but established a family home at Richmond House in Rabling Road. In his youth he was a Lieutenant in the 3rd Battalion, the Wiltshire Regiment, and then served in the Nile Expedition of 1884–85. He is buried in Swanage Cemetery at Godlingston.

Ceylon tea-planter **Henry Edward Joseph Horatio Nelson, 7th Earl Nelson (1894–1972)** retired to Richmond House, Rabling Road. He had served in the Australian Imperial Force during the First World War and with the Merchant Navy and as a Major in the Indian Army during the Second. His pastimes in his younger days were boxing and yachting. He never married.

Shipping magnate **Sir Edward Nicholl (1862–1939)** of Littleton Park, Shepperton, never forgot his humble but stimulating beginnings as an apprentice engineer on the Great Western Railway. He went on to romanticise what he called 'God's Wonderful Railway' on the grand scale, if of necessity in miniature, with his archetypal 'Model Electric Railway' with 500 feet of track at two-inches gauge, accompanied all down the line with realistic scenery, villages, towns, and an aerodrome, beside Brunel-designed viaducts, bridges and tunnels. Ostensibly for the benefit of his grandchildren, it was removed from the conservatory of his mansion – which became Shepperton Studios, the Sound City of film moguls – and brought to Durlston Castle. 'Everyone cannot but be interested in the unique collection of models which make the railway probably the most comprehensive display in this country,' to quote its 1954 brochure, picked up by the author on a childhood excursion by paddle-steamer to Swanage, after which Hornby 00-scale locomotives were never quite the same.

Adventure writer **Mary Palgrave** was one of the five daughters of Sir Reginald Palgrave of Hillside, Peveril Road, Swanage. In *Brave Dame Mary*, published in 1873, she produced a classic and typical Victorian tale with plenty of moral force, describing the heroism of Lady Mary Bankes who defiantly held Corfe Castle against its first Civil War siege in 1643. There is no shortage of condemnation of the Parliamentarians and with this kind of book selling tens of thousands of copies and running into many editions, it is hardly surprising that we were all conditioned from birth in the righteousness of the King's cause. In *Under the Blue Flag*, Mary Palgrave moved the action to Godlingston Manor, near the Ulwell Gap in the Purbeck Hills, and extended the conflicts to the Duke of Monmouth's rebellion in 1685.

The cross at the top of Church Hill, on the north side of the High Street, was erected in memory of **Sir Reginald Palgrave (1829–1904)**, the brother of Francis Turner Palgrave (1824–97) of Lyme Regis. Sir Reginald was Clerk of the House of Commons from 1886 to 1890. He had written a book on Parliamentary custom and practice in 1869 but

was better known for *The Chairman's Handbook* which appeared from 1877 onwards. He felt that the Victorian age had become hysterical, regarding his own daughter Mary as a prime example, in its and her pathological hatred for Oliver Cromwell. This he attempted to redress in 1890 with *Oliver Cromwell, the Protector: An Appreciation based on Contemporary Evidence*. Sir Reginald lived at Hill Side in Peveril Road.

Chief Petty Officer Ernest Pitcher VC (1888–1946), who was brought up in Swanage and attended its Board School, came to fame during the First World War. He was a national hero. Though severely wounded he stayed at his gun when the armed merchantman Q50, HMS *Dunraven*, engaged a German submarine on 8 August 1917. The result, from the classic Q-boat action against a U-boat, resulted in the awarding of a Victoria Cross to the ship rather than an individual. It was left to the men, in a ballot, to decide which of their number deserved it most. They chose Pitcher. He retired from the Royal Navy in 1927 but rejoined in 1939, to serve throughout the Second World War. He was also awarded the Distinguished Service Medal, the Military Medal, and the Croix de Guerre. He died at Gosport but is buried in Northbrook Road Cemetery, Swanage.

Hero's gravestone, to Victoria Cross winner Ernest Pitcher, in the old cemetery beside Northbrook Road.

Once wealthy philanthropist **William Morton Pitt (1754–1836)**, the son of John and Marcia Pitt of Encombe, near Corfe Castle, was the second of the William Pitts of the late-18th century. The first was a very different political animal, being the mastermind of the 'Pitt and Plunder' system of British Government, which created distress and poverty for his Dorset cousin to mitigate. Our Pitt, also an MP, inherited a vast fortune from his father and dissipated it on good works. Sir Tresham Lever, in *The House of Pitt*, had no doubt that it was through his spendings that 'the wealthiest branch of the family sank into the obscurity of the landless middle class'. His personal programme of social initiatives stretched across Dorset, from a fish-curing plant at Swanage and a cordage manufactory at Kingston, Corfe Castle, to a spinning and bleaching school at Fordington and a hat-making works in the new County Gaol, which he had been instrumental in rebuilding in 1787. He was the first chairman of the County Lunatic Asylum in Forston House. Somehow, through a combination of good works and bad business, he lost his great country houses at Kingston Maurward, Stinsford and Encombe as well as the village of Kingston in Purbeck. This caused him to move east, to the seaside at Swanage, where he converted the Manor House into what became the Royal Victoria Hotel. At the age of 71 he wrote: '... both Mrs Pitt and I had beggared ourselves for some time past towards the accomplishment of this object'.

Commercial educationalist **John William Ramsbottom (1885–1966)** lived at The Bushes, Durlston. He was director of the City of London College from 1925 until the end of the Second World War and then one of its governors, until 1956. He was a committee member of numerous organisations involved in industrial training. He is buried in Swanage Cemetery at Godlingston.

Art connoisseur **Sir Charles Robinson (1824–1913)**, Director of the Victoria and Albert Museum from 1852 until 1869, produced numerous publications for the South Kensington Museum, as the institution was then known. He lived at Newton Manor, at the western end of the High Street, and embellished its 16th-century rooms with Italian and other European fittings. These included doors, a staircase, shields, carved friezes dated to 1656–58, and a fish-flying weather vane which is said to have come from Billingsgate Market. Sir Charles was a frequent contributor to the arts columns of *The Times* and the *Nineteenth Century Review*.

His eldest son, **Charles Edmund Robinson (1853–1913)**, who died the same year as his father, published *Picturesque Rambles in the Isle of Purbeck* in 1882. He also wrote the *Cruise of the Widgeon*, in 1876, and several collections of poems. This Charles was a barrister. He adopted the name of the family's Swanage home, to distinguish himself from his father, being known in later life as Charles Edmund Newton-Robinson. He collected engraved gems, was an accomplished yacht racer, and sword-fenced for Britain in the Athens Olympics of 1906.

Diplomat and art connoisseur **Archibald George Blomefield Russell (1879–1955)** lived at Mount Scar House, which had been designed by Morley Horder with its owner's furniture collection in mind. He wrote standard works on *The Engravings of William Blake*, *The Letters of William Blake*, and *The Drawings of Guercino*. As Lancaster Herald at the College of Arms it was his ceremonial task to read the proclamation of His Majesty King George VI at the time of his accession in 1936.

Methodist preacher **John Sargant (1839–1930)** began preaching at Swanage before the Victorian new town of Bournemouth had its first Wesleyan chapel, and would travel there to attend its opening. He also recalled appointments on the Poole circuit which required him to walk through Ulwell and across Rempstone Heath to Ower Quay where he borrowed a boat and rowed himself across the harbour. He would return in the dark. Routine visits to far-flung congregations of just a handful of worshippers regularly involved journeys upwards of ten miles in each direction, in all kinds of weather. Though he became blind he still spent his advancing years covering most of the Isle of Purbeck. He was word-perfect in his recitation of more than 30 chapters of the *Bible* and also had the entire *Methodist Hymn Book* at the tip of his tongue.

The disc-jockey **Ed Stewart**, whose full name is Edward Stewart Mainwaring (born 1941), the son of Mr and Mrs Ray Mainwaring of South Barn, Southcliffe Road, has been a frequent visitor to Swanage. He regards himself as a Purbeck man but is not a complete native, having been born when his mother was evacuated from London, to Devon. His father, a Treasury solicitor, retired to Swanage and became a town councillor.

Colonial civil servant **Sir Theodore Tasker (born 1884)** entered the Indian Civil Service in 1908. He became Under-Secretary to the Madras Government from 1913 to 1915 and would go on to a succession of appointments in Bangalore, Coorg, and Hyderabad where he heard of his knighthood in 1937. He remained until retirement in 1944. The remainder of his life, with the former Miss Jessie Helen Mellis-Smith (1888–1974), was spent in Swanage. His final application of administrative talents was channelled into more than 20 years on Dorset County Council. Lady Tasker had already saved an important element of the town's heritage, having arranged the purchase of South Barn in 1927 and its conversion to a home by architect Morley Horder. This enhancement of Sunnydale Valley safeguarded the hinterland of what would become Durlston Country Park. Sir Theodore and Lady Tasker lived at Southover in Southcliffe Road, Swanage.

Naturalist **Leonard Spencer Tatchell (1877–1968)** of Rockleigh Cottage, Peveril Point, is buried in Swanage Cemetery at Godlingston in a position redolent of lines from his book *The Heritage of Purbeck*. He wrote that 'above, the noble hills into the afterglow of a perfect day illuminating their summits, recall the beautiful words of the 121st Psalm'. Pre-eminently a lepidopterist, Tatchell was an habitual sender and receiver of butterfly eggs and caterpillars. Many packages were none too well packed and any exotic insect found in the postal system at Swanage would be delivered to his door. Ho-You-Fat, an oriental dealer, regularly sent him Morpho butterflies from the Cayenne penal settlement in French Guiana. He then had correspondence with HM Customs in London after their interception of another Chinaman's letter 'asking if I was interested in certain drugs'. British experts in butterflies and moths frequently came to his door, and fell under the double spell of hospitality and the seaside, returning to stay for a week most summers. They included Richard South, F.W. Frohawk and Edward Step, each of whom produced standard works on their specialities.

'Sink the *Bismarck*' overlord **Admiral Sir John Cronyn Tovey (1885–1971)**, Commander-in-Chief of the Home Fleet and later Admiral of the Fleet, retired to Swanage after the war. He was created Baron Tovey of Langton Matravers in 1946. He is buried beneath a large, flat slab in Swanage Cemetery at Godlingston.

Occasional longevity was also a thing of the distant past, as was proved by **Henry Welles (1516–1607)**, of Godlingston Manor, whose brass in St Mary's Church records that he was:

... seconde sonne to Thomas Welles of Bradbridge in ye county of South [contraction for Southampton] Esqvier who being the age of 91 departed this life ye 25th of January 1607.

The brass is also to 'Marie his first wife, sister and heir to John Pole of Godlingstone Esqvier who died in Ano 1560'.

Appropriately, the alphabet has selected the town's reporter, **George Willey (born 1931)** from Cluny Crescent, to conclude this potted account of Swanage personages. He has been writing about them, and compiling his 'Tilly Whim' column, since arriving on the *Swanage Times* in time for the Queen's coronation in

Swanage reporter George Willey, who has told the town's stories for half a century.

1953. As secretary of Swanage Swimming Club he found his wife, Beata from Germany, after she almost made fatal reading by thinking that as the Isle of Wight is on the horizon it's the obvious thing to swim there. Fortunately she had been spotted by a boatman in the bay and turned back for the mainland before exhaustion set in. Cosmopolitan to the core, George became a district governor of Rotary International, and is an accomplished raconteur with a store of Swanage stories to take around Europe. He also holds court in his son Wolf's bars at the Red Lion, in the High Street, with the best gossip in town. Some of his experiences have been touched on here. He has provided details of the Iliffe murder in a house only yards from his own, and the revelation by Enid Blyton that her Mr Plod was Studland policeman Christopher Rone. George's own half an hour of fame, bringing his white goatee beard to national television, came in 1988 when he starred as reporter and editor in his own programme. He was called the 'last of a dying breed, the local man who covers everything from flower shows to the court'. The bit he recalls was interviewing a pretty girl in the nude on Studland beach. At moments like this he breathes a sigh of relief that chance career moves from his home at Newport, Monmouthshire, via the *Durham County Press*, saved him from what would have been his destiny as a Fleet Street lobby correspondent. London's loss has been Swanage's gain.

Swanage Choral Operatic Society,
conducted by David Lowe, in 1969.

Lord Lieutenant Sir Joseph Weld and Sir Arthur Bliss,
Master of the Queen's Musick, with violinist Kató Havas
from Knitson, at the Purbeck Festival of Music in 1973.

The astronomer Sir Patrick Moore on a visit to
Swanage – visibly impressed at the evidence for
an extra-terrestrial landing in the field behind.

Chapter 15

SCHOOLS AND CULTURE

The opening of Mount Scar School in 1895 with only a token child in sight.

Philanthropic reformer William Morton Pitt supported the first two Sunday schools in Swanage, which had been established in 1787, though by the turn of the 19th century schoolmaster John Stickland hardly received a salary. Then the situation changed with the arrival in 1801 of educationalist Dr Andrew Bell as Swanage rector. He brought his experiences in India, where he ran the Madras Male Orphan Asylum for Anglo-Indian offspring of the East India Company, and insisted that his 'Madras System' of pupil monitors henceforth applied in Swanage as well. Brighter youths would teach the children. 'He hammered it into us,'

Stickland complained, 'like a blacksmith on an anvil.'

Apart from this, and teaching by rote, Bell was ahead of his time. There was no cane. Good behaviour was to be achieved by encouragement and relapses deterred by detention. Stickland's colleague, Thomas Manwell, was an almost instant convert, and journeyed to London to promote the methodology. So did 13-year-old Lewis Warren, who was sent to Whitechapel in 1806, and then toured the Midlands. Lewis was an amazingly confident protégé, who by 1808 was on a boat for Barbados, assigned by the Bishop of London to experiment with the teaching of Negro slaves.

Swanage Town Band in the 1880s and 1890s, before and after beards and sashes came into fashion, in the same para-military uniform as the Dorset Artillery Volunteers.

There were now 193 scholars – just about all of young Anglican Swanage – in Bell's schools. John Stickland, however, had enough of being told how to delegate and went off to found his own school. Such small-scale day schools were proliferating and a dozen others had been set up in Swanage. Bell also saw the potential of 'industrial schools' and inspired the Cole girls, the daughters of a stone merchant, to start one so that young ladies could make straw bonnets. These would be the town's main product, apart from stone and lobsters, for the next half century, as *Kelly's Directory* recorded in 1889:

There was formerly a trade in straw plaits, giving employment to a number of women and children; it was made into bonnets, mats and other fancy articles, but the trade has declined considerably of late years.

In 1811 the initiative nationally passed to the newly-formed National Society for Promoting the Education of the Poor in the Principles of the Established Church. That snappy concept produced National Schools. Bell was their guru and the principles that applied were his but it would be the power of parochial clergy that would endure. Buckland Newton had the first National School in Dorset, in 1816, but Swanage had to wait until Victorian times.

By then, in 1837, the nonconformists had already seized the initiative locally, with the British and Foreign Schools Society setting up their British School for day pupils, with half-hearted support from independently-minded quarrymen who thought little boys should learn to 'chip stone with their hands rather than fill their heads with scripture'. It stood beside the Congregational Chapel.

The rector, Revd Thomas Oldfeld Bartlett, opened his own schoolroom in December 1836, but had reservations about the appropriate catechism to be used, which seems to have delayed National School adoption for some time. His successor would have no such theological reservations. Revd Duncan Travers, who arrived in 1854, had a philosophy that was perfect for a community of quarriers – 'build, build, build' would be the modern spin.

Schools came first on his list and the improvements and enlargements would continue at one point or another from the seaside to Herston for the next 33 years. Dorchester architect Edward Mondey was commissioned to design a purpose-built National School for Herston hamlet in 1855, in the appropriately-named Bell Street. In the middle of the town, Travers found he owned a tiny piece of glebe-land behind the High Street, beside the existing infant schoolroom at Dunford Place. Here he created another National School in 1857. Margaret Emms trawled through its records to give a time-warp account in Volume 113 of the *Proceedings of the Dorset Natural History and Archaeological Society*. In July 1872, Dr Home inspected Swanage for the Local Government Board and found that 200 children had to endure a 'sickening stench' from three privies, 'jammed into an unventilated corner', which were either connected to a blocked road drain or had no drainage at all. By this time it was being realised that typhoid and other dirt diseases were spread by such conditions.

Infectious diseases were endemic, as was absenteeism, in which the parents often colluded. The curriculum extended from religion to the natural world, via the realities of working life, as Margaret Emms shows from the Herston logbook for 1888. Objects were studied. The weather was explained. Shopping was discussed. Animals were described. Passages were learnt – giving rise to an entire generation that could recite *The Wreck of the Hesperus*.

Discipline was the stick, though the usual euphemism for this, in the records, was 'punished'. Margaret Emms found occasional references to 'flogging' in early records, with 'caning' then being used. The offences ranged from lateness and insolence to lies and violence. Thefts could lead to expulsion. Poor work might lead to spells of detention.

State education was now spreading across the land, though its arrival in Swanage was delayed with the Swanage School Board, formed in 1894, encountering determined resistance from the rector, Revd Thomas Alfred Gurney. He warned that Anglican indoctrination was under threat from a semi-secular curriculum which would return Swanage to its nonconformist roots and set the situation back by a century. Margaret Emms quotes him saying as much, that this would be 'an evil to the town religiously and financially'. Eventually, with support from the Mowlem family, London architects Houson and Houson and Swanage builders H. and J. Hardy built Mount Scar School, which opened in 1897. It was in time for Queen Victoria's diamond jubilee and the ceremony, to the rector's chagrin, was carried out by John Ernest Mowlem with a silver key. It is now displayed in the Tithe Barn Museum.

In the private sector Swanage also became a major player, starting with a small school in the Mission House in 1874, followed by a Ladies College in No. 5 Park Road in 1885, and Purbeck College in 1890. Its name was changed to Durlston Court School for the new century. Oldfeld House, in Cranborne Road, became a school and moved with its name to a green hill to the north.

Forres School was established as a boarding and day preparatory school, for boys and girls between 7 and 13 years old. Its buildings are prominent on the hilltop above the west side of Northbrook Road, north of Walrond Road, opposite Beach Gardens. The school was founded in Northwood, Middlesex, by Arthur Joseph Chadwick, in 1908, but moved to the seaside within two years. Forres was chosen to commemorate Chadwick's Elgin origins; Forres was the

Chadwick family's home town. Much extended, the present range of south-facing gable ends have grown from the 1919-dated central section, with numerous other later additions at the rear. It eventually abandoned its Scottish pedigree and went native as Purbeck View School.

Swanage Grammar School, built by Dorset County Council towards the far end of Northbrook Road, received its first pupils in September 1929. Its official opening, by the Earl of Shaftesbury, followed on 23 October 1929. Soon the roll of 160 had doubled to 320. Their first play was staged in December 1930. After the war, in 1948, a boarding house was provided for 25 boys and 25 girls, plus a gymnasium. A new woodwork room was brought into use in 1953, when the old one became a library, and a sailing club was formed in 1954. It acquired *The Spray* as its first dinghy. In 1956 a science laboratory block was added at a cost of £26 000. The four houses were St Aldhelm's, Ballard, Durlston and Peveril and dormitories were at Oldfeld House, on the hill at the north end of Walrond Road. The school closed in July 1975.

Durlston Court School had Tony Hancock as a boarder in the 1930s. Hillcrest School, dating back to 1911, moved to Carthion, which had been the home of John Mowlem Burt.

Culture also thrives at the seaside from the time of the Swanage Town Band through to the first regular moving picture shows which were established before the Great War by the Southern Cinema Company in the Cinematograph Theatre in King's Road. Talking pictures followed, in Frank Walton's Swanage Cinema, in Station Road. It had become the Grand Cinema by the Second World War.

Post-war gloom was broken by the Purbeck Festival of Music which was founded in 1954 by the accomplished violinist Kató Havas who came to live at Knitson, below the Purbeck Hills at Langton Matravers. Its genius and working figurehead was the composer Arthur Bliss who also adopted Swanage. Events continue to attract international musicians and have been held in a variety of historic settings, ranging from Smedmore House at Kimmeridge and various parish churches, including St Mary's at Swanage, to the Art Gallery at Lulworth Castle. Locally, the Swanage Choral Operatic Society was conducted by David Lowe. The potential for hosting performances and events was transformed by the reincarnation of the old Mowlem Institute as the new Mowlem venue for plays and concerts.

Herston Church of England School, founded in 1855, is now Swanage St Mark's Church of England First School, with the 1867-dated Reading Room (right) being St Mark's Pre-School.

Chapter 16

ROAD AND RAIL

It used to be said that it was easier to travel from Swanage to London by boat than to visit anywhere in Dorset. Purbeck was notorious for the appalling state of its roads. The system remained basically prehistoric, and the Roman road that must have serviced its numerous workshops and quarries had fallen into disuse at least a millennium earlier, being so totally lost that modern archaeologists talk of calling in Timeteam to find its course.

Even the first Wareham turnpike of 1768 was little improvement over the medieval road pattern as it went from Stoborough to Old Bond Street at Creech Grange. From there it linked with rough older roads to climb the Purbeck Hills at Bare Cross and approach Corfe Castle along the prehistoric ridgeway, from the west.

By the end of the 18th century a second carriage road was laid directly across the heath from Hyde Hill to Corfe Castle and then south through Corfe Common to Kingston where it made a 90-degree turn to head eastwards to Langton Matravers and Swanage. The town had been brought into direct contact with inland Dorset, in time for the invasion panics of the Napoleonic Wars. Toll-houses and gates were at the northern end of Stoborough village, facing the Wareham Causeway, and at Swanage, opposite Jubilee Road, on the High Street at Herston. Another apparently existed at Gallows Gore, although it has left no official record, where the main building was formerly called Turnpike Cottages. Charges and gates were removed in 1876.

In 1850 there was a horse-drawn omnibus through Corfe Castle to Wareham, leaving Swanage at 08.00 hours, which returned 12 hours later, daily except Sunday. George Hickson was available as a carrier on Monday, Wednesday and Saturday.

Three smacks – the *Henry, Elizabeth* and *Friends* – sailed to Poole depending on demand and conditions. A directory of 1865 shows that stone merchant Henry Gillingham was then running the 'market boat' to Poole and fishmonger William Hickson provided pleasure boats.

The course of what became the present A351 between Corfe and Herston did not become a through road until after 1862. It might have been utilised eventually by the stone trade, with steam traction engines, but the railway would come first.

Eminent Victorian architect George Edmund Street, who built the Law Courts in the Strand and a grand second church for the Earl of Eldon at Kingston, south of Corfe Castle, told a colleague about his passion for use of the 'burr', as he called Purbeck's building stone, and added: 'Let the rail or tram go to where that stone is, put it on the rail at once, and I will undertake that six churches out of seven shall be built with that material.'

George Burt, predictably, took up the cause of bringing the railway to strengthen the commercial potential of Purbeck. He held meetings to push forward the idea that the railway's coming was inevitable. Having repeated Street's words he said:

Swanage has been a place of stone for many years, but the great place now is a little to the west where there is an immense quantity of stone that could be carried to a profitable market if only they would lessen the cost of carriage. If Swanage is to move ahead and you are to get out of the dirty streets into a more wholesome and profitable atmosphere, you must have a railway.

Engineers surveyed Purbeck in 1882, and the following year – despite opposition from Wareham, the local railway town – an act was finally passed, for the second time, to bring a branch line to Swanage. There was no objection from the Earl of Eldon who owned much of the land across which it would run. Capital of £90 000 was authorised for the project and work started on 5 May 1883 at Wareham. Ten miles further on, with the date 5 May 1885, the line was completed. Robin Brasher tells me that Swanage Station was designed by quantity surveyors Galbraith and Church, to a standard LSWR design, and matches that at Bude. A year later, the Swanage branch was bought by the London and South Western Railway and the town became a holiday resort.

From the time the railway opened the seafront stone trade was doomed. The bankers were still piled with stone in 1890 but by 1905 The Parade and Institute Road had risen from their remains. Seaborne trade from Swanage ceased and one last stone barge retired to Chapman's Pool where it was left to rot. George Burt's stone-weighing office became a travel agency.

Instead of carrying stone – though the Furzebrook end still carries ball clay and now oil – the seaside end of the Purbeck branch line became a scenic holiday railway. Its special workhorses were the M7 type 0-4-4 tank engines, which ran a push-and-pull shuttle between Wareham and Swanage. They were withdrawn in 1964 and for a couple of years the line had an interesting assortment of steam locomotives that were seconded to Purbeck whilst waiting their turn to be scrapped.

From 1966 the line was worked by diesel multiple units, each of three cars, and had a particularly busy summer in 1969 as closure threatened. Public demand caused through running of trains direct between Swanage and Waterloo on summer Saturdays, the traditional hotel and boarding-house 'change-over' day, and these were packed with hundreds of passengers. Seven of these London trains are shown in one of the last timetables for the line. Each had nine or ten carriages.

After closure there was still hope of a reprieve but removal of the track with 'indecent haste' made many of us, both outside and inside the town, regard this as yet another of Dorset's lost causes. We counted without the foresight and energy of Andrew Goltz who had the vision not only to talk Dorset County Council into leasing Swanage Station to his preservation society, followed by the line itself, and then almost succeeded in bringing home the town's named mainline locomotive, *Swanage*, as their flagship. That objective slipped from his grasp, going instead to the mid-Hampshire watercress line, at Alresford. But several other ex-British Railways steam locomotives would be rescued from rust and worse at Barry Dock scrapyard in South Wales.

The rebirth of the railway has been something unique and admirable that Swanage is contributing to Dorset. Every yard of track and siding, from the seaward platform at Station Road to Norden, has had to be relaid and win the 'Light Railway Order' necessary for renovated locomotives to venture along it. Beyond, there is still a final mile, before linkage with existing track to enable through working to Furzebrook, Worgret Junction, and the main-line into Wareham.

Townspeople from Swanage, such as Jack Hardy and Mike Northover, have made sacrifices to keep progress on line, encouraged by the camaraderie of the volunteer workforce on the ground. All believe that a prime tourist county such as Dorset must be able to support a steam railway to what is one of the most highly visited pieces of coastline in Britain. The line's viability and future will be ensured the day that the first steam train since 1966 is able to take passengers the full ten miles back up the line from Swanage to Wareham Station.

Having carried more than 150000 passengers, the volunteers of the Swanage Railway could look back on a busy 2000, and membership of Southern Steam Trust – the charitable support group for their fleet of locomotives – topped 4000. They had also amassed a total of 67 non-passenger items of rolling stock and 34 passenger vehicles, including historic luxury Pullman cars which had been brought home for restoration. Paul McDonald, the operations manager, summarised the status and movements of his dozen engines during 2000. I'll paraphrase the information and include their mileages for the year, listing them in order of usage:

No. 80078 (2-6-4T British Railways Standard Class 4 steam locomotive, built at Brighton in 1954). In traffic and performing well; loaned to the Mid-Hants Railway for its October Gala. 10994 miles, over 160 days.

No. 80104 (2-6-4T British Railways Standard Class 4 steam locomotive, built at Brighton in 1955). Also in traffic and performing well. 7286 miles, over 107 days.

Blue Diesel Multiple Unit (2-engine lightweight Derby Class 108). In traffic and performing well in 2000 but withdrawn to Herston Works for a major overhaul in 2001. 6200 miles, over 125 days.

No. 30053 (0-4-4T London and South Western Railways Class M7 steam locomotive). In traffic but suffering the 'odd blown boiler tube' as it approaches 'the end of a ten-year ticket'. 5128 miles, over 84 days.

No. 34072 (4-6-2 British Railways Southern Region Battle of Britain Class named steam locomotive, *257 Squadron*, built at Brighton in 1948). In traffic, for 'Thomas' duties and 'Santa Specials'. 1798 miles, over 36 days.

No. 828 (4-6-0 Southern Railways Class S15 steam locomotive, now named for Harry A. Frith, built at Eastleigh in 1928). Withdrawn from traffic after boiler tube failures 'following a three-day period of loan to the North Yorkshire Moors Railway'. 1084 miles, over 19 days.

No. 33012 (Class 33 D6515 diesel locomotive). Decked out as *Thunderbird 2* in which guise she went out as required to rescue failed steam locomotives. 989 miles, over 41 days.

Green Diesel Multiple Unit (4-engine, 2-coach lightweight Derby Class 108). Back-up coaches, in traffic as required. 926 miles, over 19 days.

No. 35027 (4-6-2 British Railways Southern Region Merchant Navy Class named steam locomotive, *Port Line*, built at Eastleigh in 1949). Withdrawn for tube-plate repairs for most of the year but brought back into service for winter 2000. 407 miles, over 8 days.

Swanage Station, newly opened in 1885, with engine number 209, its fireman, driver and line-up of staff.

Signal Box, with British Railways 0-4-4T engine number 30111 pulling out of Swanage Station, with a train for Wareham, at 14.43 hours on 9 September 1954.

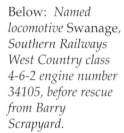

Left and below: *Brighton-built in 1954, type 2-6-4T British Railways standard class 4 engine 80078 'reserved' for the Swanage Railway at Barry Dock, in 1973.*

Below: *Named locomotive* Swanage, *Southern Railways West Country class 4-6-2 engine number 34105, before rescue from Barry Scrapyard.*

Above: *Engine Shed entrance, with an ex-Midland Railway tank engine emerging (0-6-0T class 1F, number 41708).*

The arrival of 80078, turning from Shore Road into Victoria Avenue on 23 September 1976, heading for Swanage Goods Shed and renovation in the Herston Workshop.

Austerity-class locomotive Joseph *on the turntable.*

No. D3591 (Class 08 diesel shunter). General work-horse around Swanage Station, being 'an under-rated star, working hard on carriage washing and general shunting'. 288 miles, over 44 days.

No. 41708 which has also carried the number 41712 (0-6-0T Midland Railway Class 1F steam locomotive). In service in February. 209 miles, over 4 days.

No. D9521 (Class 08 diesel shunter). Used by the Permanent Way Department in track re-laying, currently in the vicinity of former clay tramway bridge No. 13, east of Catseye Bridge carrying the main road across the lifted section of line at Norden. 148 miles, over 9 days.

No. 30075 (0-6-0T Southern Railways USA Class steam locomotive, built at Vulcan Iron Works in 1943). Out of service awaiting boiler repairs.

A century ago, it was the failure of Edwardian transport initiative that saved the Isle of Purbeck from what would have been suburban sprawl on a mega-scale and congestion at Studland to turn every afternoon into a bank holiday Monday. This was the final scheme by the Burt family of Swanage to improve Purbeck's communications which was killed by small-town politics in Poole and Bournemouth. It was an ambitious but commercially viable idea for conveying tramcars across the water between Sandbanks and Shell Bay by means of overhead cables. The *Bournemouth Graphic* reported, in 1904:

We are enabled to publish this week the official announcement that the plans and arrangements for an important development of the tramway system to Canford Cliffs and Swanage are practically complete. This is the first announcement that has been made on the matter, and we are in a position to give authentic details of the scheme in so far as present arrangements permit.

A private company has been formed, and among those taking a prominent part in its working, we believe, are Sir John Burt of Swanage, and Mr Bankes, of Corfe Castle, to establish a system of trams, which will start from the Westbourne Arcade, and run through Seamoor Road and Branksome Park, across Canford Cliffs to Sandbanks. Here it is proposed to erect a tower on either side of the water, and by means of a cable and chain arrangement to swing the cars across to the opposite bank and thence continue the system to Swanage. We understand that it has not yet been decided whether the line of the route will pass through Studland, though the whole scheme is complete in all but one or two minor details.

The capital of the company is to be £68,000, and we are informed that practically the whole of this sum has already been privately subscribed. No appeal will therefore be made to the public.

In the event, it would be the Floating Bridge chain-ferry that would carry cars and passengers across the mouth of Poole Harbour, and National Trust ownership of most of Studland parish since 1982 now holds the line against futuristic solutions.

End of the line, at Swanage, as 257 Squadron *awaits scrambling.*

*The Swanage Railway as busy as it gets, with engine 30053 on the turntable (top right),
an optimistically-headed 'Grantham' train in the siding (left), Battle of Britain class engine 34072,
named for 257 Squadron (centre), and Austerity-class* Wilbert *also in steam (foreground).*

*No. 30053 (as Thomas the Tank Engine) in steam in front of No. 34072 (257 Squadron)
between the Engine Shed and water-tanks below Northbrook Road Bridge.*

No. 30053 being manoeuvred, literally, on the turntable beside the Engine Shed.

Practicalities of coaling and watering for Battle of Britain class locomotive No. 34072 (left) below Northbrook Road Bridge with No. 30053 waiting on the turntable (sporting the lion emblem of nationalised British Railways).

Austerity-class locomotive **Wilbert** *(aka Percy, work-mate of Thomas) heading
a five-coach train pulling out of Swanage Station for Corfe Castle.*

Chapter 17

WAR AND WARFARE

The prisoner-of-war camp at Ulwell, drawn by Fred Hibbert at the end of the Great War.

To put Swanage and warfare into context, a millennium after shipwrecked Vikings, in 1855 William Masters Hardy and his friends assembled on Peveril Point to watch the British fleet under sail for the Crimea. They counted them out and watched the survivors return, heading for Portsmouth, after peace was proclaimed with Russia in April 1856. That was the excuse for a patriotic party on Peveril Downs with musicians playing and an exotic orange and large twopenny bun for each child.

Peveril Point Battery, the town's historic defensive position on the promontory between Swanage Bay and Durlston Bay, was established in 1558 and rebuilt in 1774, with stone and turf barbettes, in a semi-circular arc, beside a stone-built Watch House. Its notional armament was six guns in time of war, including two or three from the wreck of the *Halsewell*, with a view towards the Isle of Wight and into the English Channel, where France was the traditional enemy over the horizon. The guns fired 4-inch cannon balls weighing 5lbs.

The practice ground for Infantry volunteers was in Sentry Field, between Seymer Road and Park Road to the west of Peveril Downs, evolving into use of a Watch and Preventive Station, in the ownership of William Morton Pitt, until 1836. This Custom House later became Rookery Court, and then The Rookery,

taking its name from the nests in tall elms which had been planted by Pitt's predecessor, John Dampier, the last row of which was felled in 1898.

Swanage was at the fore as a front-line observation post in 1803, as invasion was feared and Emperor Napoleon himself was widely believed to have slipped into Lulworth Cove, though the story can be shown to be unfounded. In the couple of years before the Battle of Trafalgar set the country at ease, about 120 volunteers gathered each Sunday in Ship Lane, Swanage, and marched towards Peveril Point. Known as the 'Sea Fencibles' – after the Fencible Light Dragoons, who were disbanded in 1800 – they were pikemen rather than gunners. Their organiser was Nathan Chinchen who mustered them in what became known as Marshall Road.

A Royal Navy signal station was in operation on Round Down, some 600 yards north-west of Anvil Point, during the Napoleonic Wars. It relayed shore to ship messages by telegraph, on the system devised by Sir Home Riggs Popham, and then by semaphore using a great upright hoarding of circles and squares like an oversized cricket scoreboard. The foundations of a walled enclosure on Round Down, with six ancillary buildings, can be traced. They are grouped together around a depression about 18 feet by 20 feet that marks the site of the signals apparatus.

Left: *Victorian field guns on Peveril Point, looking westwards towards the Clock Tower and 1859-built pier, in the early 1870s, before building of the Lifeboat House.*

Right: *'Swanage Bay from Peveril Point' in an engraving by Philip Brannon, dated 1 August 1856, which shows the fort with cannon (right), The Grove (left), and the pier with steamer (centre).*

No. 5 (Swanage) Company of the Dorset Garrison Artillery, standing to attention at Peveril Point Battery in about 1890, with an obsolete weapon and its cannon balls from Nelson's day.

Dorset Infantry Volunteers, at their summer camp at Whitecliff Farm, 1905.

Swanage Company of the 1st Dorset Garrison Artillery
Volunteers, on winning the King's Cup after the Boer War.

The historic site was at the seaward end of Peveril Point but a position facing the town, immediately east of the Coastguard Station, was earmarked by the War Office for re-occupation by Dorset Artillery Corps – part of the backbone of Victorian home defence – in 1868. The *Yeovil Gazette's* Swanage correspondent reported from the town in April 1869:

An Artillery Corps has been formed here. Fifty-five members were sworn-in on Monday and afterwards marched to Herston and back. Mr J. Pope is Hon. Secretary to the Corps. Lord Eldon and Mr G. Burt have granted leases of the ground necessary for a battery and for carbine practice.

By 1880 the Corps was 40 strong and 'some very good firing with the big guns was made at the floating signal in the bay'. The target was a barrel moored on the Tanville Ledge where divers have found 6-inch cannon balls weighing 26lbs. Two artillery pieces of this calibre were kept in the Drill Hall and dragged out amid much local excitement for practice shots.

On the other side of the town, on 'alms-land of Ulwell' at Whitecliff Farm, a Volunteer Camp of the full county complement of the Dorset Rifle Volunteers met in July 1868 and July 1873, and then returned regularly until Edwardian times. The eastern fields became a mass of white tents set out in a dozen rows, with an officers' mess, officers' reading tent, hospital, privates' mess tent, and a ladies' cloak tent for visitors. The riflemen even brought their own printing press on to the field and produced a daily camp newspaper entitled the *Swanage Spider*, which started by explaining how they came to the seaside:

The field in which the tents are pitched is on a gentle declivity towards the sea, and terminates by a precipitous cliff overlooking the lovely beach. The field, which is about 11 acres in extent, has been kindly lent for the purpose by Mr Isaac White, of White Cliff Flax Mills. Adjoining this is a meadow, also lent by Mr White, in which the sutlers' [camp workers] camp is found; and the drill ground contiguous [immediately to the west] is a large field, 17 acres in extent, placed at the disposal of the Battalion by Mr Samuel Hunt, of Godlingston Farm. The prospect obtained from the camping ground is magnificent, the cliff which forms a kind of natural gallery around the amphitheatre of the bay, giving a peculiar advantage to the spectator.

Anecdotes record recurrent local difficulties with the Dorset intellect and language:

Whilst the Battalion were drilling yesterday a worthy Sergeant Instructor put the following question to a recruit: "What are you, front or rear rank?" "Narne o'nt." See Johnson's Dictionary or somewhere else.

In 1873:

... the same fat-headed reptile that was prowling about the refreshment tents the first time we camped here, crawled up before the officers and looked smiling upon me, and then he leered at the officers and said: "This man is not drunk".

Some knowledge of the politics of the time would be useful in solving this riddle. 'When the Ministers have finished their whitebait dinner at Greenwich, and lighted their cigars, what bathing place will the Chancellor of the Exchequer be like?' The answer is given under the heading 'Quantum stuff' and is Lowestoft. You need to recall that Robert Lowe was Gladstone's Chancellor and progress to 'Lowe stuffed'. Other shades of humour are timeless: 'All women ought to be dear to men. Some are – very!' Ethnic minorities were already an easy target: 'A Black Man Wanted. If he has a tail he would be preferred. Apply at Pandemonium, Dorchester line.'

Charles Powell wrote a song, 'The Volunteers are Ready,' which was sung to the tune of 'Auld lang syne' and has the famous split infinitive of a century later – 'To boldly go' – excused in both cases by euphony:

The Volunteers are ready now;
And wait our country's call
To boldly go, and beat their foe,
Or in the struggle fall.

We'll conquer; or we'll die my boys,
We'll conquer or we'll die;
Thus freely meet a soldier's death,
And there in glory lie.

Swanage features in this fragment from *The Camp-fire King* by Colour Sergeant E.T. Budden, to the tune of 'Le Petit Tambour':

Nor would we Swanage Bay forget,
For boats and bathing rare;
Nor all the fun of tented life,
Nor Drew's substantial fare!

Yes, we'll pile up the faggots high,
And wake the jocund song,
For the Camp-fire comes but once a year,
And does not tarry long.

Many veterans of Edwardian camps would be among the first to be enlisted and find themselves going to France with the British Expeditionary Force after Europe found itself at war on 4 August 1914. The war was only over by Christmas for doctor's son

Captain Philip Ernest Viney of the Leicestershire Regiment and Cintra, in Swanage, who 'died for England' at Bailleul on 17 December 1914. Commander Rolf Viney RNA survived the First World War but died shortly afterwards, at the age of 37, on 22 April 1922.

Swanage found itself back-stage at Armageddon. Throughout the First World War, Dorset No. 36 Voluntary Aid Detachment ran the Red Cross Hospital at Cluny, in Cluny Crescent, on the southern slopes of the town. The large house was leased from the trustees of Kenneth Anderson. It opened in the early months of war, on 9 November 1914, and remaining operational until after the Armistice, closing on 15 January 1919 when its stores, valued at £127.5s.6d., were donated to Swanage Cottage Hospital. Its honorary secretary was A.J.B. Unwin.

With 50 beds, it initially treated the sick and wounded from a tented camp established at Swanage for Kitchener's Army, receiving 231 patients in 1914. In 1915 there were 851 admissions but the camp's own hospital opened in November that year and Cluny's 318 cases in 1916 were mainly from overseas, having been transferred for recuperation from Christchurch Hospital and Cornelia Hospital, Poole. The numbers were 311 for 1917 and 272 for 1918.

Because critical and surgical cases were not generally admitted the death rate was low, totalling just three for the entire period it was open, and all of these occurred in 1915. Two died from cerebral meningitis and the other had pneumonia.

The hospital had a busy war, according to its closing report:

Under the Matronship of Sister Henry, the Hospital gained a great reputation with Tommy as a happy place, where he was well fed, comfortably housed, and his medicine and surgical needs carefully attended to. Discipline was well maintained, and the advantage of this was felt when in 1918 a fire broke out at the hospital, and was only prevented from becoming very serious, by the prompt action of Orderly Hibbs, aided by the patients, who fought the fire successfully.

There was also an RAF Hospital, established towards the end of the First World War for convalescent cases, where 29-year-old Captain Clement Perronet Sells died on 4 July 1919 from an illness contracted on active service. Lieutenant-Colonel Leslie Jenkins of Swanage, who had gone to France with the Royal Flying Corps, was another casualty. He was killed on 1 April 1918, shortly after the RFC was re-titled the Royal Air Force.

Nurses and convalescent patients at the Red Cross Hospital before closure after the end of the First World War.

143

The other evacuees of war to the seaside at Swanage were Germans, to an extensive Prisoner-of-War Camp on Bankes Estate land at Ulwell. Its collection of timber huts remained in use for more than a year after the Armistice in 1918.

Offshore, it had been a busy war, with U-boat sinkings including the 4383-ton merchantman *Kyarra* off Durlston Head on 5 May 1918, at the start of what should have been a voyage from Southampton to Sydney. On the personal scale, naval casualties of the First World War included Gunner Ernest Northover on HMS *Tipperary*, Able Boatman P.J. Pesel on the cruiser HMS *Hampshire*, and Leading Seaman Frederick C. Tomes on the battleship HMS *Barham*. Able Boatman Leonard Wicks and Coast Guard Percy Milverton also failed to return home.

The town had a local hero, from its very own Board School, who, as previously mentioned, was chosen for the nation's highest honour by the unusual process of a democratic vote among his comrades. The crew of HMS *Dunraven*, disguised as armed merchantman *Q50*, were told their vessel had been awarded the Victoria Cross for engaging and sinking a German U-boat on 8 August 1917. They chose 29-year-old Chief Petty Officer Ernest Pitcher, who carried on firing his gun while seriously wounded, as the individual to receive it on their behalf. Their daring attack was described by Lieutenant-Commander Harold Auten VC as 'the greatest action of any Q-boat against a submarine. It was fought by a ship's company of heroes.'

The battleships HMS *Barham* and HMS *Malaya*, both of 31 100 tons and mounting eight 15-inch guns, sailed into Poole Bay in September 1919 and anchored for the duration of the Schneider Trophy races which attracted elite flyers from all over Britain and war-torn Europe. Swanage should have had the best view as the circuit for the sea-planes had its turning point off Durlston Head. In the event the so-called winner, Guido Jannello, found himself lost in fog and turned instead at a buoy in Studland Bay.

Out of the gathering clouds between the wars the Astra Show of Sir Alan Cobham's Flying Circus descended on Swanage, on 14 August 1934, with aeronautic stunts that would be enacted for real with eight-gun fighters in 1940.

Enemy mines claimed numerous losses in local waters in 1940, killing 11 volunteer members of the Royal Navy in HMS *Abel Tasman* in the Swash Channel approach to Poole Harbour on 13 June 1940. British mines and obstacles were laid along Swanage beach in July 1940 and the old and new Victorian piers were 'broken' at their landward ends, by the Royal Engineers, to prevent them being utilised by German invaders. Some 200 feet of supports and decking were blown-up. The defences were manned initially by the

Grenadier Guards and then the Royal Welch Fusiliers. The White House became the local Air Raid Precautions and Home Guard base. Check-points were established across coastal approach roads – the High Street beside the stone quay; Institute Road; Station Road; Victoria Avenue; Walrond Road; and with a fortified and mined roadblock beside the Waterworks at Ulwell. Among the emplacements for 40-mm Bofors anti-aircraft guns was the flat roof of Hestercombe which is now the Cumberland Flats.

Anti-invasion bunkers and gun batteries, with underground communications cables, were constructed on the seaward side of Godlingston Farm. Coastal radar stations were built to detect E-boat incursions and co-ordinate anti-ship guns. A secret network of Operational Bunkers of the newly-formed Auxiliary Units of British Resistance were underground Nissen huts, set in holes and covered with timber and camouflage. From these the fight could be continued from behind enemy lines if the enemy came. Guerrilla warfare training took place at Duntish Court, Buckland Newton, and in the nearby wilderness of Melcombe Park.

Swanage was on the front line throughout the Battle of Britain. The first British casualty was a Spitfire of 609 Squadron from RAF Warmwell, near Moreton, on 8 July 1940. Spitfire R6634 from the same squadron was claimed by the gunner of a Junkers Ju.88 bomber on 18 July. The RAF came off badly in a prolonged dog-fight off Durlston Head on 20 July with 152 Squadron from Warmwell losing a Spitfire. Supporting them were the Hurricanes of 238 Squadron from RAF Middle Wallop which lost P3766. Sergeant-Pilot Cecil Parkinson died from extensive burns, after being shot down into the sea, and 501 Squadron also lost a Hurricane at Swanage.

Trying to repel the second Luftwaffe attack of the day on Convoy CW9, as it broke through the enemy blockade heading down-Channel from the Thames, two fighters of 152 Squadron from RAF Warmwell ran out of ammunition and headed for home. They were intercepted by Messerschmitt Bf.109s over Swanage and riddled with bullets. Both pilots had close shaves. Sergeant-Pilot Denis Norman Robinson brought Spitfire K9894 down in a forced landing on meadows at Bestwall, near Wareham. The aircraft bounced into a ditch and came to a stop standing vertically, minus a wing, with its propellers embedded in the mud. Denis Robinson was able to jump down on the ground, as did Flight-Lieutenant Pilot Officer Beaumont, after bringing his Spitfire down at Spyway Farm, overlooking the cliffs at Langton Matravers.

Nearly killed over the town, on 25 August 1940, was Polish Spitfire pilot Piotr Ostaszewski-Ostoja

Many Second World War flying-boat pilots, operating from Poole Harbour for BOAC and the RAF, had trained on City of Swanage *which was the principal training aircraft of Imperial Airways in the 1930s.*

As well as the 'Big Red One' the 1st Infantry Division of the United States Army – which occupied Swanage in the spring of 1944 and invaded Omaha Beach – was also known as the 'Fighting Firsts'.

D-Day returnees to Swanage on the 50th anniversary in 1994. Native-born Ron Turner of the British Army poses beside an American Sherman tank and Lieutenant-Colonel Don Helgeson of the United States 1st Infantry Division adjusts his glasses beside its 'Big Red One' emblem.

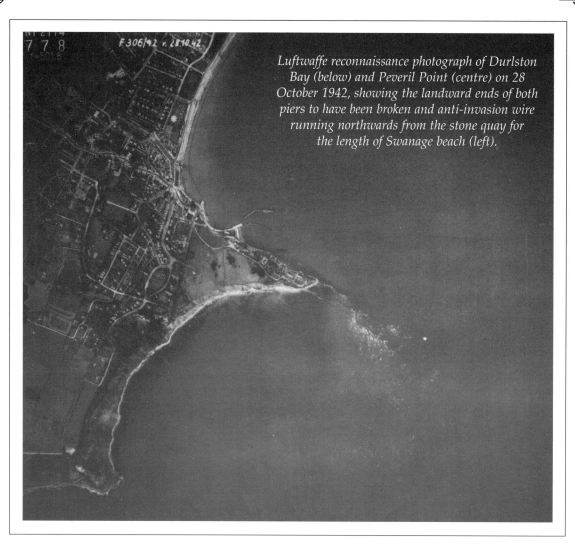

Luftwaffe reconnaissance photograph of Durlston Bay (below) and Peveril Point (centre) on 28 October 1942, showing the landward ends of both piers to have been broken and anti-invasion wire running northwards from the stone quay for the length of Swanage beach (left).

Coastal gun batteries on Peveril Point, manned by the Royal Artillery, engaged German E-boats – fast motor gunboats – which harassed Allied shipping in the English Channel.

of 609 Squadron. His fighter was riddled by cannon fire from a Messerschmitt Bf.110, with one of the shots going through his arm, but he managed to escape and crash land the crippled fighter through the perimeter hedge of Warmwell Aerodrome. He went on to have a reasonably good war, retiring from the RAF as Wing Commander, and changed his name to Peter Raymond on deciding to stay in Britain.

Less fortunate was Sergeant Pilot John McBean Christie, in Spitfire K9882 of 152 Squadron from Warmwell, who was shot down off Swanage by Messerschmitt Bf.109 fighters as he tried to intercept some 60 Heinkel He.111 bombers that had wrecked the Supermarine Works at Woolston, Southampton, on 26 September 1940. On 30 September 1940, after an interception with Green Section of 609 Squadron from Warmwell at 23 000 feet over Swanage, a Messerschmitt Bf.109 was put down into the sea off the Isle of Purbeck. It was claimed by Pilot Officer Michael Appleby. The following day the Luftwaffe had its revenge when Flight-Lieutenant Charles Earl Bowen and Sergeant Pilot Norman Brumby, in Hurricanes of 607 Squadron from RAF Tangmere, were shot down and killed over Swanage Bay in a dog-fight with Messerschmitt Bf.110s.

One of these engagements was watched by Brian Sharpe, now living in Tunbridge Wells, who told me:

On a Sunday afternoon I recall a Spitfire came low over the bay and town with engine spluttering and crashed through a hedge at Ulwell, close to Godlingston brickworks. I believe the pilot was killed.

Among those delighted to step ashore in wartime Swanage was Flying Officer Edward 'Jumbo' Deansly, from the town's RAF Air-Sea Rescue launch, on 26 September 1940. It had been his second ducking in the month, when his Spitfire of 152 Squadron from Warmwell was shot down into the English Channel, 12 miles south of The Needles. On the previous occasion he had been picked up by a freighter and put ashore at Lyme Regis. He went on to fly night-fighters and would survive the war, having been promoted to Wing Commander.

German bombs fell regularly on Swanage through the Second World War, with hit-and-run raids from the Luftwaffe, operating from bases only 70 miles away on the occupied Cherbourg peninsula. Several left death and destruction.

On 20 April 1942, houses were damaged in Cromwell Road, as were commercial buildings in Station Road. Bomb damage was sustained by historic and picturesque Wesley's Cottage, in the High Street, on 14 May and would cause its demolition. Three people were injured on 13 July when houses were damaged in and around Park Road.

Eight people were killed and 39 wounded on 17 August 1942 when the Westminster Bank at No. 1 Institute Road suffered a direct hit and was destroyed.

Among the dead was the bank's 53-year-old manager Horace Albert Mills. Miss Helen Muspratt's photographic studio at 10 Institute Road was badly damaged, as was Hayman's Café. Bombs also fell in The Narrows – devastating the constricted terraces of old cottages that formed the characterful pinch-point in the middle of the High Street – and in Chapel Lane and Church Hill. Cottages opposite the old parish churchyard were ruined and tiles ripped off St Mary's Church. There was also damage to the nearby Tithe Barn. German bombs had destroyed Paradise on Church Hill which would become the site of the post-war rectory.

Five people were killed and nine wounded on 23 August 1942 when extensive damage was caused to commercial buildings around The Square. The most dramatic casualty, however, was inanimate. The monumental terracotta cow that formed the centre-piece to the façade of Swanage Dairies fell in pieces as the building collapsed into a heap of rubble. The adjoining Ship Inn also suffered considerable damage.

Military occupation was everywhere. Holiday towns in wartime are full of spare space. Visitors included the young man who became Professor Sir Bernard Lovell of Jodrell Bank telescope fame. He was one of the 200 scientists and their assistants who came to Worth Matravers in May 1940 with the Telecommunications Research Establishment who would win the Battle of the Beams and go on to develop the radar intercepting and pathfinder devices of the secret war. He was sent to Swanage, he told me years later, on the day when he made a sentimental return to his seaside home at No. 38 Rabling Road: 'It was newly built and I numbered it myself by pacing out the empty building sites. There were several of us living there.'

By the time they left, in May 1942, some 2000 were employed in huts and requisitioned buildings from St Alban's Head to Langton Matravers. There were fears that the Bruneval raid, bringing back enemy radar apparatus, would be reciprocated by a German commando raid in Chapman's Pool. 'Churchill ordered that we left and said that we had to go before the next full moon,' Sir Bernard said. He then put the capabilities of my camera flash into cosmic perspective: 'The radio energy received by the 250-foot Lovell telescope over a period of 1000 years would light a torch lamp for just one second.'

The spectacular finale to Purbeck's war took place with Exercise Smash on Studland Beach in a live-fire rehearsal for the invasion of Normandy. Detachments of the United States 1st Infantry Division – the 'Fighting Firsts' who were also known as 'Big Red One' from their badges – occupied much of Dorset, including the Hotel Grosvenor, and would be destined to take Omaha Beach in the bloodiest landings on D-Day. The royal train arrived in Swanage on 17 April 1944 and King George VI dined at the Hotel Grosvenor, the local headquarters building for the following day's manoeuvres, with Field Marshal Sir Alan Brooke (Chief of the Imperial General Staff), General Sir Bernard Montgomery (effectively commander-in-chief Allied land forces, commanding the British 21st Army Group), and Lieutenant-General Miles Dempsey (commanding the Second British Army).

Their wake-up call would be 04.00 hours on 18 April for a particularly loud Tuesday. Police had toured Swanage telling people to leave open all their windows – to minimise blast damage – before naval and aerial carpet and pattern bombing commenced at dawn, and the town vibrated to the thud of full-scale war across the hill. The VIPs were taken to Fort Henry, an immense observation bunker on Redend Point, behind Studland Manor. Assault landings followed, also with munitions, from small-arms fire to rockets.

Dating from the evening before D-Day, the largest single relic of Swanage at war is the 7-ton anchor of the French battleship *Courbet*, which lies off Durlston Head. It had to be slipped to enable her to be removed from what would be her penultimate storm, on 5 June 1944, when she was under tow. The big ship's engines and boilers had been stripped in preparation for her use on the Normandy coast as a 'Gooseberry' blockship. Instead she was filled with concrete. En route, however, she hit heavy seas and was forced into the lee of the Purbeck cliffs. When the time came to weigh anchor and resume her tow, to the final resting place, the vessel had no power with which to lift the anchor, so it had to be released. After placement in France, later in the month, the blockships and Mulberry Harbours suffered some displacement from another fierce storm.

At the personal end of the scale, bringing tragedy rather than drama, wartime telegrams continued to confirm worst fears. A prisoner of the Japanese, Henry James Chinchen, died in Sandakan Camp, North Borneo, on 14 April 1943. He was the 29-year-old son of Frances and Harry Chinchen from one of the oldest Swanage families. The 'Roll of Honour' for Swanage Grammar School records the names of Haydn Newman of the Royal Navy; Edward George Brindle of the Royal Marines; John Lewis Henry Mouland of the Fleet Air Arm; Ronald Cecil Parker of the Army; Michael William Cockbaine, Bernard Denness, Stanley James Honour, Leslie Newman, George Nicol, Arthur Dennis Slade and William Brian Wheelwright of the RAF; and civilians Kathleen Winsome Hawkins and Cyril James Smith.

'Known unto God,' Rudyard Kipling's inspired phrase for the unknown victims of war, applies to three Merchant Navy men whose bodies were brought ashore and buried in Swanage Cemetery at Godlingston. Their bodies were recovered on 3 June, 18 July and 19 September 1942. There is also 'A Soldier of the Second World War' with his stone dated 8 July 1944.

The minefield at Swanage was one of the last in Dorset to be cleared. It was initially classified as 'too dangerous to clear' by 21-year-old Lieutenant Ralph Ruby of the Royal Engineers. Ruby and Lieutenant Rex King led a BD (Bomb Disposal) team eastwards into Purbeck, after having blown up more than 3000 mines at Ringstead Bay alone; a fraction of the number laid along this coast in a desperate measure to disrupt German invasion in 1940. By 1947, as their work drew to a close, they regarded themselves as a 'happy team' in contrast to their colleagues elsewhere who made news with high attrition rates from lack of judgement.

Swanage would be their exception, but not until a fateful Friday the 13th, in May 1955. One of the mines that was missed by the clearance teams had been discovered by a group of 20 boys from Forres Preparatory School. King and Ruby had reported in 1948 that 'a discrepancy of 58 mines exists' but this was ignored and the beach declared safe.

Five boys were killed in Britain's worst land-mine disaster, in a rock pool below Shep's Hollow, at the northern end of the beach. The mystery object was shaped like a farm cheese. The lads clustered around as one of them prodded the rusty steel cylinder. There was a huge explosion and one of the victims was totally blown to pieces, with only one of his shoes being recovered – which was identified by 'a brass school number 29 punched into the side'.

Two boys were wounded. They and other survivors, including Robert Key who would become Tory spokesman on landmines in the Major Government, had to endure weeks of explosions as the Sappers returned to complete the task of clearing 'the forgotten minefield'.

On 5 April 1982, Swanage watched as the Empire prepared to strike back, with word spreading through the town that Operation Corporate was under way with the aircraft carriers HMS *Hermes* and *Invincible* being clearly visible from Peveril Downs, outward bound to rendezvous with two-thirds of the fighting strength of the Royal Navy. They were heading for the South Atlantic, leading a Task Force which would form as a Battle Group off Ascension Island, to head for the Antarctic and recover the Falkland Islands in an operation worthy of Nelson. As with the Victorian warships that went to the Crimea, Swanage would witness the safe return of Rear Admiral Sandy Woodward's flagship, HMS *Hermes*, towards the Isle of Wight and Portsmouth at the end of the Winter War.

Chapter 18

GHOSTS AND FOLKLORE

Haunted Godlingston Manor.

Purbeck traditionally receives the first cuckoos in the county, often in the first week of April, and dependably in time for Wareham Spring Fair which used to be held on 17 April. 'There', it was said, 'he buys himself a pair of breeches'. Most parishes in south-east Dorset have their Cuckoo Pen or Cuckoo Pound, attached to small and often wooded enclosures. These date from the 18th century or earlier and usually seem to be next to former areas of common grazing rights. There is one south of Verney Farm, a hundred yards west of the Swanage boundary in the parish of Langton Matravers. This small wood has the only trees on the central stone plateau of southern Purbeck and lies midway between South Farm and Blackers Hole, half a mile from the sea.

It was a general belief, before and indeed after the time of naturalist parson Gilbert White, that cuckoos, like swallows, hibernated in hollow trees. Logically – always a perilous quality to bring to folklore – they were first heard in the Cuckoo Pounds, and therefore believed to have over-wintered there. Another bit of the reasoning is that before falling into disuse and becoming overgrown, these enclosures had their origin as stock pounds for bullocks and hogs being gathered for the Cuckoo Fair, as it was called, at Wareham. Cuckoo Fair Pounds became Cuckoo Pounds as

fair-going declined. The bird's association with the event came about because it is the reliable audible clock for the first couple of weeks in April.

Tom Burnham's Oak marks the site of a suicide burial, probably with a stake through his heart to lay the ghost, which took place as custom dictated beside the highway, at what was then a crossroads on the parish boundary. He was from Langton Matravers and is buried beneath an oak tree at an old road junction near Godlingston, at the parish boundary between Langton Matravers and Swanage. Burnham had hanged himself. Despite the unmarked grave, his name persists around the spot, with Tom Burnham's Oak standing beside Burnham's Lane.

It intrigued me as an inquisitive child that there were two junctions in Burnham's Lane and I asked folk-tale author Olive Knott, in Sturminster Newton, to tell me which had the legends attached to it. She sent me a letter from George Clark of Steer Road, Swanage, written in 1961:

I attended Herston School fifty years ago and the lanes and fields close by were our playgrounds. The particular oak is quite fifty yards from the crossroads. The tree bore the deeply cut initials T.B. for Tom Burnham. The limb on which he tied the rope had long since been sawn off as was the usual custom. A story rife at that time was that Tom was buried under the green mound at the crossroads, but some said it was the burial place of a witch, a wooden stake having been driven through her body. Whilst on the subject of burials outside consecrated ground a few years ago a skeleton was dug up in a quarry at Langton. It was only four feet below the surface. At an inquiry it was held to be the remains of a coloured man, no doubt washed ashore nearby. Presumably a colour bar operated in those days and he was not deemed a fit subject to be buried in the local church yard.

A later instance of a suicide's burial – long after 1823 when the law banned the custom of staking and other mutilations of the corpse – was that of John Ball, landlord of the Ship Inn at Langton Matravers. The licensed premises were then in the cottage nestling beside the three-storey inn which replaced it on the summit of Steps Hill in 1884. John Ball had parted from his wife, Mary Holmes Ball, but the couple agreed to call a truce and spend Christmas together in 1878. The arrangement fell apart a week before that, on 18 December, when they had what was to be their last row, after closing time. Mary ran home to her mother's cottage as John followed with a shotgun. He blasted the front door as she locked it against him. She was unhurt but John turned around and returned to the public room in the Ship where he blew his head off.

Langton's rector, Revd Lester, protested at the sequel, in which because he was declared to be 'felo-de-se' – felon of himself – by an inquest jury, John Ball 'was buried like a dog' beside the highway at 21.30 hours on the night of 22 December 1878. 'He wanted his wife to come and live with him,' Lester wrote, continuing:

She felt she could not. Life then appeared so black to him that he shot himself. If he was sane, why be so cruel to survivors, so uncourteous to a poor dead man; seeing that to him prayers could mean nothing, and even a suicide's burial nothing, while to them the touching service might have been of vital importance. We do hope that verdict will be the last of its kind in our neighbourhood.

It was as a result of the rector's letter-writing campaign that the 'crime of suicide' was mitigated by two Acts of Parliament, in 1880–82, to allow its victims to be buried in a churchyard as if they had died a natural death.

Such events, and the echoes of past violence, are carried down to us through folk memory. Jean Bowerman, living in Godlingston Manor, recorded the story of its ghost in 1967, when she was able to add her own psychic experience. She had been told of the apparition of a lady who was supposed to walk beside the garden wall, and recalled:

... seven years ago, I think, she decided to look in through a window when I was working late. I didn't see her, but had I been a dog, my hair would have stood on end as I felt her presence. Not appreciating the feeling, I fled.

Mrs Bowerman gradually forgot her experience until a former occupant of Godlingston came to tea. Conversation turned toward the ancient window and the woman said that her husband had once seen a ghostly face, staring in, in broad daylight. Then, she said, the lady vanished. Following the visit, Mrs Bowerman became more spectrally aware:

Now, alas, the ghost has come inside and seems to have taken a fancy to the upstairs landing and she's even more of a deterrent than the slugs to going down at night. Not that I'm afraid – let's just say that I prefer not to look behind me on the landing.

Newton Cottage, now known as Heather Close, also has its ghost story. A blaze there on 11 December 1966 was said to have 'something of a ghostly nature' though Chief Fire Officer R.E.J. Paull provided a more prosaic explanation: 'It could have been caused by someone sleeping rough and leaving a cigarette end behind, or perhaps, by children playing with matches.' Ghosts, real or imagined, were invoked by Swanage parents to discourage their impressionable offspring from places regarded as potentially dangerous. The house had been left in a time-warp, fully furnished with made-up beds, on the death of photographer William Cox and that of his widow. They had left no family. The fire, by whichever agency it was caused, was confined to a single room and stairway.

Springfield House is also haunted, or at least the third of it named Mulberry Cottage, which became the home of Sara Robinson and Rob Grindon. They traced its history back to brewer Peter Marsh who rebuilt the house at the end of the 17th century. Sara, a spiritual healer, became convinced that she was hearing window shutters being bolted and doors shutting. A friend saw a bottle of wine fall from a rack. Another visitor was emphatic that he had seen the figure of a woman pass through a wall, at a point where there was a blocked doorway, of which he was unaware. Strong smells came up from under floorboards in the front room. The building featured in a BBC television series, the *House Detectives*, directed by Samira Osman.

Investigators were also told, as is said of just about all of them, that the mulberry tree was planted by King James I in 1603. The true twist to the legend is that James ordered their planting, thinking of a species used for making silk, and country house owners sensibly planted black mulberries instead – for their juicy fruit – which were useless for silkworms. As for the Swanage tree, dendrologist John White determined that it dated from 1828.

Chapter 19
HERITAGE AND HABITATS

Classic Walter Pouncy shot of Swanage in 1890s, with Swanage Bay and Whitecliff Farm (foreground) with the fields between it and the photographer now being National Trust owned and holding the line against advancing suburbia.

Much of any history concentrates on time's casualties but there is much that has survived into the third millennium. Swanage remains well endowed both scenically and architecturally. Gems in the built environment include the quaint group of survivals on the east side of Church Hill, just below Sir Reginald Palgrave's memorial cross. The curving terrace comprises The Arc, Wyvern Cottage, Georgian Cottage and then numbers 4 and 2 Church Hill. 'W.C. 1793' is the keystone above the arch of the alleyway between Wyvern Cottage and Georgian Cottage but the stone has '1940' added below, as a reminder of wartime bomb-damage repairs.

Durlston Country Park, covering 270 acres of the south-eastern extremity of Swanage and Purbeck, was created by Dorset County Council in 1974. It was the first country park in Dorset and was the

direct result of Alan Swindall's initiative, as County Planning Officer, who visualised the former Victorian and Edwardian outdoor playground being given new life in a 'careful balance between people and nature'.

His foresight and the subsequent enlisting of an 800-strong band of volunteers, known as the Friends of Durlston, led to an award citation from English Nature in 2000. 'Watching the park develop has been a worthwhile experience,' said head ranger Hamish Murray:

The Friends have been a real thrill to work with. They are actively involved in most aspects of the site, from surveying to seeding new hay meadows, stone-walling, general maintenance, computer input of records, and staffing the visitor centre.

Fine landscape photograph by Colin Graham, in 1985, of National Trust cliffs from Belle Vue westwards to East Man, above Seacombe.

An estimated 400 000 visitors pass through the park each year, with a quarter of those going to the visitor centre where they can monitor nesting birds, via closed-circuit television cameras. Hydrophones pry on the private lives of the dolphins in the waters off Durlston Head and Anvil Point. Here the Lighthouse is another draw, and a steady flow of walkers continue westwards, along the coastal path. Less adventurous visitors have Durlston Castle and the Great Globe. Cliff quarries called Tilly Whim Caves – the best-known Victorian attraction – remain off-limits after rock-falls, though you can still look down on an often angry sea from stone-walled paths with their idiosyncratic series of inscriptions including poems, scripture, and the height above sea level.

Despite the weight of human traffic, Durlston boasts over 400 species of native wild flowers, including nine types of orchids. These are suitable food-plants for 30 species of breeding butterflies. They include the chalkhill blue, brown argus, and Adonis blue. Ten species of grasshoppers and bush-crickets can be heard and seen in the turf and scrub. Half the landscape is relatively close-cropped, by a herd of 20 or 30 young beef cattle, but the remainder is left to nature and varies from windswept cliffs to impenetrable scrubland. Migrating breeding birds cross the coastal pastures in spring and autumn. Guillemots, razorbills and peregrine falcons breed on the cliffs.

Making the award in 2000, English Nature's Victoria Copley paid tribute to the achievement of Alan Swindall's vision for a successful 'balance between the requirements of nature conservation and the needs of thousands of visitors'.

The long-running friction between ornithologists and climbers has been smoothed by a compromise that creates sanctuaries and areas with closed seasons but allows unrestricted access elsewhere. Some of the climbs rank amongst the most popular in the country and the classic ones have their own names, including Rendezvous Manque between Durlston Head and Tilly Whim Caves, and Traverse of the Gods between the caves and the lighthouse. At the side of the headland is the Subliminal Cliff. West of Anvil Point are Via Christina, Nutcracker Exit, Marmolata Buttress, Sheerline, Bottomless Buttress and Boulder Ruckle Exit.

Westwards, the next-door landholding is at Belle Vue Farm, where the National Trust was given 51 acres of orchid-rich clifftop fields in 1976 through a donation from Mr L. Forder in memory of his wife, Mrs E.A.E. Forder. These cliffs form the south-western corner of Swanage parish and are still being farmed in a way that George Gill would recognise from a century ago. Below, inaccessible apart from by sea, is Half Moon – a rocky cove – which is named for its shape.

Northwards, linked to the other lands by public paths, a 32-acre corner of the former quarrylands above the High Street was saved by Dorset Naturalists' Trust – now renamed Dorset Wildlife Trust – and is accessible as the wonderful wilderness of Townsend Nature Reserve. On the other side of the town, onwards and upwards from Whitecliff Farm to the northern boundary running along the spine of Ballard Down, the National Trust acquired another 222 acres using its Enterprise Neptune appeal funds in 1976. The farm buildings, not included in the acquisition, have a 1683 date-stone which has been re-set in a barn. Strip lynchets survive, though in poor condition, in part of a former open field which used to extend to the foot of the steep downland slope. These medieval strips were worked as cultivation terraces.

The entire length of the hilltop has a contiguous boundary with land on the Studland side of the parish boundary which the Trust would inherit in 1982, following the death the previous year of Ralph Bankes who turned out to be its greatest ever benefactor. As well as his home and art collection he had bequeathed the entire 16 000-acre Kingston Lacy and Corfe Castle Estates. This consolidated the Trust's hold of the backdrop to the Swanage view, along Ballard Down to the Ulwell Gap, Godlingston Manor and Godlingston Farm, and beyond the Purbeck Hills across almost the entire parish of Studland to Poole Harbour and Brownsea Island, which it already owned. Westwards the Trust found itself owning Verney Farm, with the Swanage parish boundary running between its fields, and in 1994 acquired adjoining coastal downland at Spyway Farm, including the rocky shelf of Dancing Ledge, linking with the next block of Bankes land at Eastington and Seacombe.

The visible effect of Trust ownership on high-profile parts of the landscape has been to turn back the clock. Arable farming for cereals has been stopped along Ballard Down and chalk downland restored, though it will take decades for the former orchid-rich turf to reinstate itself. The bonus has been the removal of the hilltop fence which is now superfluous as a boundary.

The older Mowlem name is perpetuated by de Moulham Road in Swanage and the de Moulham wall-snail, which had one of its last British habitats run over by the Newbury bypass in the early 1990s.

A mystery name is California Farm, for an 18th-century house in the coastal hinterland a mile south-west of Swanage, beyond the quarrylands, between Herston and Round Down. It is probably an ironic allusion to its inaccessibility, being in the far west of the parish and reached by an indirect stony track, as a literal translation of California is most unlikely. For that, from the Spanish, means 'hot furnace', which however much I talk of 'sunny Swanage' would be something of a climatic exaggeration.

153

View to the east from Belle Vue Cliffs, showing benign waves rippling along the Ragged Rocks.

SOURCES AND BIBLIOGRAPHY

Anonymous, *The ABC Guide to Swanage*. Fifth edition, Bournemouth, 1919.

Anonymous, *Durlston Castle, Swanage, Dorset*. No imprint, circa 1954.

Anonymous, *Mary Burt went for a Walk: The Story of Purbeck Methodism*. Parkstone, 1974.

Austen, John, editor, *Purbeck Papers*. London and Poole, 1852–69.

Baker and Sons, Durlston Park Estate, Swanage. London, 1891.

Bartelot, Richard, *Princess Drina comes to Swanage*. Corfe Castle, 1983.

Bowerman, Jean. Information on Godlingston Manor's Ghost. Personal interview and *The Farmer's Weekly*, 29 September 1967.

Brannon, Philip, *The Illustrated, Historical and Picturesque Guide to Swanage and the Isle of Purbeck*. Fourth edition, Poole, 1869.

Braye, John, *Swanage*. Second edition, London, 1890.

Calkin, J. Bernard, *Ancient Purbeck*, Dorchester, 1968.

Chacksfield, Merle and Bob. Encouragement, hospitality, and information on myriad matters. Personal interviews, 1984–2001.

Chacksfield, K. Merle, *Swanage at War*. Swanage, 1993.

Colvile, Frederick Leigh and John Clavell Mansel, *Brief Notices of Purbeck*. Unpublished manuscript, 1853.

Emms, Margaret, 'Education in Swanage,' *Proceedings of the Dorset Natural History and Archaeological Society*, Volume 113. Dorchester, 1991.

The Exton Hotels Company Ltd, *Hotel Grosvenor Swanage: Souvenir Tariff*. Swanage, undated.

Guttridge, Roger, *Dorset Smugglers*. Second edition, Wincanton, 1987.

Hardy, Thomas, *The Hand of Ethelberta: A Comedy in Chapters*. First edition, London, 1876.

Hardy, William Masters, *Old Swanage or Purbeck Past and Present*. Two editions, Dorchester, 1908 and 1910.

Hardy, William Masters, *Smuggling Days in Purbeck*. Dorchester, 1907.

Hardy, William Masters, *Wave Action on our Coast*. Dorchester, 1911.

Haysom, David, and Bragg, David, *Swanage and Purbeck in Old Photographs*. Stroud, 1991.

Haysom, David, and Patrick, John, *Swanage in old picture postcards*. Zaltbommel, 1992.

Heath, Sidney, and Hazlehust, Ernest, *Swanage and District*. London, circa 1910.

Holland, Clive, *The Gossipy Guide to Swanage and District*. London, circa 1905.

Hutchins, John, and subsequent editors, *History and Antiquities of the County of Dorset*. London, three editions, 1774 to 1874.

Jeaffreson, John Cordy, *Victoria: Queen and Empress*. London, 1893.

Kelly's Directories Ltd, *Kelly's Directory of Dorsetshire*. London, editions for 1889, 1915, 1935 and 1939.

Land Agents' Record, reprint from, entitled 'The Durlstone [sic] Park Estate, Swanage, Dorset.' London, 6 June 1891.

Legg, Rodney, *Dorset Flight: The Complete History*. Wincanton, 2001.

Legg, Rodney, *Dorset National Trust Guide*. Wincanton, 1992.

Legg, Rodney, *Literary Dorset*. Wincanton, 1990.

Legg, Rodney, *Mysterious Dorset*. Second edition, Wincanton, 1998.

Legg, Rodney, *Old Swanage*. Milborne Port, 1983.

Legg, Rodney, *Purbeck Island*. Two editions, Milborne Port, 1972 and Wincanton, 1995.

Legg, Rodney, *Swanage Encyclopaedic Guide*. Wincanton, 1995.

Legg, Rodney, *Wartime Dorset: The Complete History*. Wincanton, 2000.

Legg, Rodney, editor, *Dorset, The County Magazine*. Milborne Port, 1968–84.

Legg, Rodney, editor, *Purbeck, The Country Magazine*. Tiverton, 1999–2001.

Lewer, David. Information, principally on the Burt and Mowlem families. Personal interviews and various publications listed here, 1975–2001.

Lewer, David, *Hardy in Swanage*. Wincanton, 1990.

Lewer, David, *John Mowlem's Swanage Diary*. Wincanton, 1990.

Lewer, David, *The Story of Swanage*. Bournemouth, 1986.

Lewer, David, and Calkin, J. Bernard, *Curiosities of Swanage or Old London by the Sea*. Fourth edition, Swanage, 1999.

Lewer, David, and Smale, Dennis, *Swanage Past*. Chichester, 1994.

Makin, William J., *The Life of King Edward the Eighth*. London, 1936.

Mitchell, Vic, and Smith, Keith, *Branch Line to Swanage*. Third edition, Midhurst, 1992.

Nash, Paul, *Dorset Shell Guide*. London, 1936.

Parsons, Jack, *Princess Victoria in Dorset, July and August 1833*. Bournemouth, undated.

Pitfield, Fred, *Hardy's Wessex Locations*. Wincanton, 1992.

Pitfield, Fred, *Purbeck Parish Churches*. Wincanton, 1985.

Robinson, Charles Edmund, *A Royal Warren: Picturesque Rambles in the Isle of Purbeck*. London, 1882.

Royal Commission on Historical Monuments, Dorset Volume II, parts 2 and 3. London, 1970.

Swanage Brick and Tile Co Ltd, *The Manufacture of Hand Made Bricks*. Swanage, with boxed specimens of seven types, undated.

Swanage News, Swanage Railway Society newsletter. Swanage, 1976.

Swanage Railway News, Swanage Railway Project magazine. Quarterly editions, Swanage, 1988 onwards.

Swanage Spider, Camp newspaper. Daily editions, Swanage, 1868-73.

Swanage Tramway and Pier Act. London, 22 & 23 Victoria, Session 2, 1859.

Tatchell, Leonard, *The Heritage of Purbeck*. Dorchester, circa 1955.

Tringham, Sidney, *The Bollard Story*. Swanage, 1975.

Urban District of Swanage, *Building Byelaws*. Swanage, 1939.

Willey, George. Scintillating conversation with gossip masquerading as briefings on contemporary happenings. Personal interviews, 1968–2001.

SUBSCRIBERS

Brian W. Adams, Twickenham, Middlesex
Shirley and John Albin, Swanage, Dorset
Alan and Roza Aldridge, Swanage, Dorset
Bryan Anders, Swanage, Dorset
Alexandra Anderson, Studland, Dorset
W. G. Andrews
Mr Michael D. Angell, Swanage, Dorset
June Appleton, Swanage, Dorset, 1975
A. C. and D. A. Armstrong, Swanage, Dorset
J. Peter Arnold, Great Hale, Lincs.
P. Ashton, Swanage, Dorset
Gillian C. Baggott, Swanage, Dorset
James Bangle, Swanage, Dorset
John Bannister, Perth, Western Australia
Judy Barcham, Swanage, Dorset
Irene M. Barlow, Swanage, Dorset
Olive J. Barrow, Swanage, Dorset
The Barrows, Peveril Point
Jean Bartlett, Swanage, Dorset
Mrs Audrey Beall, Merley
Trevor Betts, Brockham, Surrey
Nigel Beviss, Wool, Dorset
Fay Beviss, Florida, USA
Daphne E. Billington, Swanage, Dorset
Brian and Minwell Bird, Cardiff
Bertram H. Bishop, Swanage, Dorset
Phyllis Bishop, Swanage, Dorset
Mr and Mrs Jack Bornoff, Wellesbourne, Warwickshire
Andrew D. Bracey, Ruislip, Middlesex
Mr B. Bradford, Swanage, Dorset
Malcolm D. Breach
R. M. Brewer, Swanage, Dorset
Patricia M. Brindley, Swanage, Dorset
Peter Britton, Fordingbridge
Arthur H. Brown, Swanage, Dorset
David J. Brown, Swanage, Dorset
Gillian Brown, Swanage, Dorset
Mrs Elsie Browne, Queens Road, Swanage, Dorset
Philip and Joan Bruton, Swanage, Dorset
Nick Buckland, Swanage, Dorset
Judy Bugler, Worth Matravers, Swanage, Dorset
Andrew Travers de Jersey Burnet, Peveril Point,
    Swanage, Dorset
Diana Burrell, Swanage, Dorset
Bob and Carol Burt, Swanage, Dorset
Martha A. Calderon, Swanage, Dorset
Bob Campbell, Swanage, Dorset
Sue Carter, Swanage, Dorset
Lee A. Carter, Swanage, Dorset
Mrs K. M. Chacksfield, Swanage, Dorset
Crosby Chacksfield, Sidford, Devon
Roger Chacksfield, Medstead, Hampshire
Malcolm P. Challis, Swanage Caravan Park
Dr John Challis, Swanage, Dorset
Linda J. Chalmers (née Smith), Swanage, Dorset
David Brian Chellingworth, Weymouth, Dorset
Michael J. Chinchen, Swanage, Dorset
Doris E. Churchill, Studland, Dorset
Patricia Churchill, Swanage, Dorset
Clifford Churchill, Swanage, Dorset

Krysia Ciupek, Corfe Castle, Dorset
Dennis A. Clark, Swanage, Dorset
Richard Clarkson, St Paul's Cray, Kent
David and Sheila Clements, Swanage, Dorset
Heidi Clements and Andrew Clarke, Swanage, Dorset
David and Linda Cleverly, London
Jennifer Coates, Swanage and Oxford
Patricia Gill and Malcolm Cole, Swanage, Dorset
Wynne and Gordon Collins, Swanage, Dorset
Denis Ian Compton, Wheathampstead, Herts.
Mr Roderic Cooke, Swanage, Dorset
David Corben, Swanage, Dorset
R. and M. Cory, Swanage, Dorset
Pam Cousins, Swanage, Dorset
Reg and Val Covil, High Wycombe
Mrs M. A. Cowell, High Street, Swanage, Dorset
Helen Creer, Indianapolis, USA
P. Crowe, Bournemouth
Peter J. Curran, Purbeck Court, Swanage, Dorset
Faye Curtis, Swanage, Dorset
Roger and Sarah Deakin, Studland, Dorset
Mr and Mrs N. Dean, Aldershot, Hants.
D. G. Dean, Swanage, Dorset
David J. Deas, Swanage, Dorset
James N. Denholm, Manor End, Swanage, Dorset
Peter Denness, Swanage, Dorset
Sandie Denty, Swanage, Dorset
M. L. J. Dexter, Radlett
Eric P. M. Dorrington, R.A.F.V.R.
Sylvia Yvonne Downton
Mr M. and Mrs J. Duckett, Twyford, Berkshire
William Duffield, Harmans Cross, Swanage, Dorset
H. M. Duffy, Swanage, Dorset
Sylvia Dunford, Dover, Kent
Peter Dunning, Gomersal, West Yorkshire
Len and Juliet Eden, Churlston Ferrers
R. and P. A. Edmunds, Swanage, Dorset
W. A. Edwards
Dennis H. Edwards, Swanage, Dorset
Gerald M. Edwards, Swanage, Dorset
Lois and Rod Eggington, Andover, Hants.
Bill Elliott and family, Swanage, Dorset
The Ellwood family, Swanage, Dorset
Terry and Caroline Ely
Ron and Sandy Emmitt, Harmans Cross, Swanage, Dorset
John Errington, Swanage, Dorset
Adrian N. Fidler, Swanage, Dorset
Renee E. Fidler, Swanage, Dorset
C. J. Figg, Swanage, Dorset
Christopher G. Finch, Redbourn, Herts.
Marion and John Fletcher, Swanage, Dorset
Peter and Judy Fontes, Parkstone, Dorset
Gerald T. Fooks, Swanage, Dorset
Nora K. Fooks, Swanage, Dorset
Jill Fox, Bracklesham Bay, West Sussex
Peter Gibb, Swanage, Dorset
Captain Alex W. R. Gibbons, Swanage, Dorset
Leslie Gibbons, The Owl Pottery, High Street,
    Swanage, Dorset
Jean Gibbs, Swanage, Dorset

SUBSCRIBERS

C. J. Ginger, Swanage, Dorset
Sheila and Barry Glendening, Horseshoe House Hotel, Swanage, Dorset
Olive Goldstone, Welwyn Garden City
Christine P. Gould, Swanage, Dorset
David S. Gould, Swanage, Dorset
Andrew M. Gould, Swanage, Dorset
Brian J. Graham, Swanage, Dorset
Angela J. Grant, Swanage, Dorset
David Greene, Harlow, Essex
Christine Grimshaw, Grays, Essex
June Hannam (née Harding), Swanage, Dorset
Brenda M. Hardy, Boscombe, Dorset
John S. Hardy, Longthorpe, Peterborough
Ronald James Hardy, Swanage, Dorset
Dot Harries, Swanage, Dorset
Derek Harris, Codicote, Herts.
Beryl and John Harris, Langton Matravers, Dorset
David and Christine Harrison, Cliff Top Care Home, Swanage, Dorset
Robert and Hester Dora Harrison, Virginia, USA
Brenda Harvey, Swanage, Dorset
Andrew Hawkes, Poole, Dorset
Revd John Hawkins, South Croydon, Surrey
Julie Hazlett, Waterlooville, Hants.
H. J. and Y. J. Heath, Hoburne Park, Swanage, Dorset
Anne and Sidney Highwood, Swanage, Dorset
Mrs Julie Hill, Swanage, Dorset
Mr John Hixson
Chris and Joan Hoad, Swanage, Dorset
Russell Hobbs, Prospect Smallholding, Swanage, Dorset
Colin Hoddinott, Poole, Dorset
Stephen J. Holley, Swanage, Dorset
Terry and Jean Holloway, Swanage, Dorset
Rose Hopley, North Baddesly, Hants.
Stanley and Nancy Hornsby, Swanage, Dorset
Bernard Howells, Swanage, Dorset
Phyllis D. Jackson, Swanage, Dorset
Moira Walker and Michael Jacobs, Swanage, Dorset
Jane A. Jenkins, Welling, Kent
Ann Johns, Swanage, Dorset
Daphne Johnson, Swanage, Dorset
Eric and Edith Johnson, Saddleworth, Yorkshire
Mrs Jasmine C. Joyner, Swanage, Dorset
Mrs Mary Karlberg, Kalmar, Sweden
Dean A. Kelly, Swanage, Dorset
Geoff Key Kenilworth, Warwickshire
Barry Kerr, Bournemouth
Michael and Anne King, Wareham, Dorset
Steve and Lynn King, Swanage, Dorset
Maureen L. Knott, Hertford, Herts.
Jonathan P. Lander, Worth Matravers, Dorset
Alan Lander, Worth Matravers, Dorset
Fiona A. Lander, Swanage, Dorset
Kirsty A. Lander, Swanage, Dorset
Richard and Hilary Lane, Northbrook, Swanage, Dorset
Stan E. Leach, Swanage, Dorset
Colin D. Lee, Calcot, Berkshire
Leeson House Field Studies Centre, Langton Matravers, Dorset
D. Legg, Swanage, Dorset
K. Legg, Swanage, Dorset
Simon Lewty, Swanage, Dorset
Ann Lillington (née Chinchen), Clevedon, Somerset

The Limes Hotel, Swanage, Dorset
Frederick Linley, Swanage, Dorset
The Littleton family, Swanage, Dorset
Josephine Lobley, Swanage, Dorset
P. Lovell, Swanage, Dorset
Roger and Sally Lunn, Lindfield, West Sussex
Lyons, Swanage, Dorset
Janet A. Lyons, Swanage, Dorset
Julie MacDonald-Olds, Alberta, Canada
Drs Brenda and Ian Maddick, Thame, Oxon
Keith Marlow, Swanage, Dorset
Graham Marshallsay, Alresford, Hampshire
Michael MccGwire, Swanage, Dorset
Cameron McGlone, Twickenham, Middlesex
Warwick and Jessica McGlone, Kinross, Western Australia
Victoria McGlone, London
Cameron McKinnon, Dundee
Dr Peter Merrett, Swanage, Dorset
K. Moore, Swanage, Dorset
Dora Moore, Swanage, Dorset
Jack and June Morrell, Swanage, Dorset
Tim and Caroline Morris, Swanage, Dorset
James R. Morrison, Durlston, Dorset
Peter and Barbara Mortimer, Swanage, Dorset
Mr and Mrs Laurie Moss, Swanage, Dorset
Nigel and Bobbie Motley, Grange Park, London
Jeffrey A. C. Mowlam, Dorchester, Dorset
Ian Murdoch, Swanage, Dorset
Barrie and Lynne Murray, Woking, Surrey
Mr William T. F. Nash
Daphne D. Nash, Swanage, Dorset
Margaret B. Needs, Swanage, Dorset
Janet Norgate
Barry and Carol Norman, Swanage, Dorset
Michael Norman, Clevedon and Mount Misery
Dr and Mrs K. J. O'Reilly, Swanage, Dorset
Mark O'Reilly, Swanage, Dorset
Michal Olizar Wolczkiewicz
Anthony Orchard, Swanage, Dorset
Winifred Orchard (née Green), Swanage, Dorset
John Orr, Swanage, Dorset
Trevor Ottewill, Swanage, Dorset
Tim and Tina Parsons, Swanage, Dorset
Roger Parsons, Swanage, Dorset
C. G. and I. E. Parsons, Studland, Dorset
Hilary Passmore, Swanage, Dorset
J. and P. Paul, Swanage, Dorset
Daphne and Dennis Pearson, Hemel Hempstead, Herts.
Margaret Perkins, Swanage, Dorset
David B. Perry, Langton Matravers, Dorset
Mrs Patricia Pharaoh, London SW17
Martin and Anne Phippard, Warminster, Wilts.
Jacqueline B. Pike
Richard Pilcher, Cerne Abbas, Dorchester, Dorset
Elizabeth M. Pilkington, Swanage, Dorset
Mrs I. F. Pinchbeck, Wimborne, Dorset
Chris and Sylvia Pippard, Vanscoy, SK, Canada
Mary Platford, Andover
Margaret A. Powell, Bristol
Tony Poyntz-Wright, Taunton
Gary and Karen Prescott, Swanage, Dorset
Group Captain Basil Primavesi, Studland, Dorset
Mrs W. J. Raison, Swanage, Dorset
Lorna and Stuart Randall, Exeter, Devon

June Ranger, Swanage, Dorset
Maureen Redko, Swanage, Dorset
G. Martyn Rhead, Swanage, Dorset
Richard T. Riding
Eric A. Roberts, Swanage, Dorset
Frank E. Roberts, Swanage, Dorset
Ken R. V. Rodger, Swanage, Dorset
John and Sue Rowntree, Court Farm House,
    Swanage, Dorset
S. Rowsell, Pinnacles Reach, Swanage, Dorset
R. G. Ruffell, Swanage, Dorset
District Judge Mark Rutherford, Bath
Mrs Alison Rutherford, Bath
Peter M. Ryan, Swanage, Dorset
James and Mary Sabben-Clare, Corfe Castle, Dorset
Suzanne and Grant Sadler, Colchester, Essex
Harold Samways, Swanage, Dorset
Michael I. Scott, Swanage, Dorset
David G. Scott, Swanage, Dorset
Roy E. Selby, Crossways, Dorset
Teresa M. M. Sheppard, Martinstown,
    Dorset/formerly from Swanage
Mary Sims, Ballard Estate, Swanage, Dorset
Kathleen Smith, Swanage, Dorset
Jeremy F. Smith, Swanage, Dorset
Roger H. Smith, Swanage, Dorset
Robert D. Smith, Swanage, Dorset
Lesley M. Smith, Swanage, Dorset
Wendy and Roy Smith
Doug and Marie Smith, Swanage, Dorset
Kenneth J. Smithson-Downes, Swanage, Dorset
Y. Spindler-Don, Swanage, Dorset
Jean and Ron Spradbery, Swanage, Dorset
Lynda Stacey, Castleton Hotel, Swanage, Dorset
Susan and Max Stanford, Swanage, Dorset
Charlotte J. Stares, Swanage, Dorset
Steve and Dave, The Old Water Tower, Swanage, Dorset
Michael A. Stollery, Swanage, Dorset
Geoff Styles, Studland, Swanage, Dorset
Bill and Anne Summers, Studland, Dorset
Marian Suttle, Gillingham, Dorset
Bernard and Monica Sutton, Swanage, Dorset
Derek (Spud) Taylor, Swanage, Dorset
Wayne Taylor, Swanage, Dorset
Mark Taylor, Swanage, Dorset
Mrs Patricia A. Thompson, Swanage, Dorset

Mr and Mrs R. Thompson
Michael and Susan Thorpe, Harman's Cross, Dorset
Pippa Tierney, Swanage, Dorset
Mrs Geoffrey Tomes
Bernard Tomes, Wareham, Dorset
Noel E. and Alison J. Tomes, Guildford, Surrey
Tower Lodge Hotel, Swanage, Dorset
Paul Treasure, Swanage, Dorset
The Truman family, Swanage, Dorset
M. J. Turner, Acton, Langton Matravers, Swanage
Robert D. Turner, Swanage, Dorset
Nathan S. Turner, Swanage, Dorset
Margaret and Jim Urquhart, Swanage, Dorset
The Van de Zande family, Swanage, Dorset
Miss Zöe and Hannah Varney, Swanage, Dorset
Les and Margaret Vaudrey, Irlam
Mrs Y. D. Wadkins, High Street, Swanage, Dorset
Sue and Barrie Waldron, Swanage, Dorset
June Walker, Swanage, Dorset
John F. W. Walling, Newton Abbot, Devon
Jim and Barbara Walsh, New Duston, Northampton
David and Sue Ward, Broadstone
Pete and Lyz Warn, West Knighton, Dorset
Angela K. Waterman, Studland, Swanage, Dorset
Margaret Rosamund Watkins, Swanage, Dorset
Geraldine A. Watkins, Swanage, Dorset
Barbara J. Watson, Swanage, Dorset
Rex G. Webb, Swanage, Dorset
P. Webb (née Goater), West Sussex
Susie Weeks, Cornwall
Mark and Liz Welch, Taunton, Somerset
Haydn and Nicky Welch, Taunton, Somerset
Sheila and Bob West, Swanage, Dorset
Peter F. Western, Corfe Castle, Dorset
David J. White, Swanage, Dorset
Richard J. Wickens, Swanage, Dorset
Martin and Joan Wickham, Swanage, Dorset
Barry Wiggins, Swanage, Dorset
Iain Wilkie, Islington, London
Rosemarie Williams, The Black Swan, Swanage, Dorset
Audrey Williams, Swanage, Dorset
Daphne Windrum
Mr and Mrs R. Wiseman,
Mrs J. Wyatt, Swanage, Dorset
Sue Younghusband, Hitchin, Herts.

The water-wheel at Swanage Mill, already picturesque rather than functional, when Alfred Dawson sketched it in 1882.

ALSO AVAILABLE IN THE SERIES

The Book of Addiscombe • Various
Book of Bampton • Caroline Seward
Book of Bickington • Stuart Hands
Blandford Forum: A Millennium Portrait • Various
The Book of Brixham • Frank Pearce
The Parish Book of Cerne Abbas • Vale & Vale
The Book of Chittlehampton • Various
The Book of Constantine • Moore & Trethowan
The Book of Cornwood and Lutton • Various
The Book of Creech St Michael • June Small
The Book of Cullompton • Various
The Book of Dawlish • Frank Pearce
The Ellacombe Book • Sydney R. Langmead
The Book of Grampound with Creed • Bane & Oliver
The Book of Hayling Island and Langstone • Rogers
The Book of Helston • Jenkin with Carter
The Book of Hemyock • Clist & Dracott
The Book of High Bickington • Avril Stone
The Book of Ilsington • Dick Wills
The Book of Lamerton • Ann Cole and Friends
Lanner, A Cornish Mining Parish • Scharron Schwartz
& Roger Parker
The Book of Loddiswell • Various
The Book of Lustleigh • Joe Crowdy
The Book of Manaton • Various
The Book of Meavy • Pauline Hemery
The Book of Morchard Bishop • Jeff Kingaby
The Book of Minehead with Alcombe • Binding & Stevens
The Book of North Newton • Robins & Robins
The Book of Paignton • Frank Pearce
The Book of Pimperne • Compiled by Jean Coull
The Book of Plymtree • Tony Eames
The Book of Porlock • Denis Corner
Postbridge – The Heart of Dartmoor • Reg Bellamy
The Book of Priddy • Various
The Book of Rattery • Various
The Book of Silverton • Various
The Book of South Stoke • Various
South Tawton and South Zeal with Sticklepath • Roy and
Ursula Radford
The Book of Sparkwell with Hemerdon
& Lee Mill • Pam James
The Book of Stithians • Various
The Book of Torbay • Frank Pearce
Uncle Tom Cobley and All: Widecombe-in-the-Moor •
Stephen Woods
The Book of Watchet • Compiled by David Banks
The Book of West Huntspill • Various
Widecombe-in-the-Moor • Stephen Woods
The Book of Williton • Michael Williams
Woodbury: The Twentieth Century Revisited • Roger Stokes
The Book of Woolmer Green • Various

SOME OF THE MANY FORTHCOMING TITLES

The Book of Addiscombe, Vol. II • Various
The Book of Barnstaple • Avril Stone
The Book of Bridestowe • R. Cann
The Book of Buckland Monochorum • Hemery
The Book of Carshalton • Stella Wilks
The Book of Chagford • Ian Rice
*The Book of Chittlehamholt with
Warkleigh & Satterleigh* • Richard Lethbridge
The Book of Chittlehamholt with
The Book of Colney Heath • Bryan Lilley
The Book of Down St Mary • Various
*The Book of Dulverton
with Brushford, Bury & Exebridge* • Various
The Book of Dunster • Hilary Binding
The Book of Hurn • Margaret Phipps
The Book of Lulworth • Rodney Legg
The Book of Markyate • Richard Hogg
The Book of Mawnan Smith • Various
The Book of Newdigate • John Callcut
The Book of Newton Abbot • Ian Rice
The Book of North Tawton • Various
The Book of Northlew with Ashbury • Various
The Book of Peter Tavy • Various
The Book of Publow with Pensford • Various
*The Book of Sampford Courtenay
with Honeychurch* • Stephanie Pouya
The Book of Staverton • Pete Lavis
The Book of Studland • Rodney Legg
The Book of Wythall • Val Lewis

For details of any of the above titles or if you are interested in writing your own community history, please contact: Community Histories Editor, Halsgrove House, Lower Moor Way, Tiverton Business Park, Tiverton, Devon EX16 6SS, England, e-mail: sales@halsgrove.com If you are particularly interested in any of the images in this volume, it may be possible to supply a copy. Please telephone 01884 243242 for details.

*In order to include as many historic photographs as possible in this volume, a printed index is not included. However, the Community Histories are currently being indexed by Genuki. For further information and indexes to volumes in the series, please visit:
http://www.cs.ncl.ac.uk/genuki/DEV/indexingproject.html*